Memoirs of a Mystic;

In Training

Melissa Amos

Copyright 2023 Melissa Amos.

All rights reserved

Memoirs of a Mystic; In Training

No part of this book may be reproduced, distributed, or transmitted in any form or by any means without the prior written permission of the publisher, except in the case of brief quotations embodied in critical reviews and certain other noncommercial uses permitted by copyright.

Some parts of this book have been fictionalised, or names changed, for various purposes and to protect the individuals involved.

This book is not intended as a substitute for medical advice or intervention.

All ideas and opinions are the authors own.

For Molly-Nana;

Thank you for your wisdom, your love, and your words,
and how they have flowed into mine.

For all Mystics in Training;

"A little magic can take you a long way."
- Enid Blyton, "The Faraway Tree"

May these words help you discover the mystic that lies within.

- Melissa Amos

A Note From The Editor

Memoirs of a Mystic is a book that has opened my mind in so many ways.

I have been on my own spiritual journey for the last 13 years and have a strong working knowledge of many aspects of this topic. However, not only did Melissa, introduce me to topics that I was unfamiliar with, she also was able to present existing wisdom from a fresh perspective that really caused some inner shifts for me.

Helping Melissa to bring this book together and subsequently proofread and edit has helped me to explore more of who I am with real love and acceptance.

Each time I have read it, I feel as though I have gained some new knowledge that serves me in the moment. I know that this book will touch your heart and soul.

It is a roadmap home to the one true place that matters- yourself.

Katie Oman - Editor, and Author

Praise for The Book

"We are all **Mystics in Training!** Learning to connect to inspiration, living a guided life, making yourself instrument for a higher purpose, and being a loving presence in the world.

Melissa's delightful memoir offers wonderful insights and help for your journey. Enjoy!"

- Robert Holden, author of Higher Purpose, Shift Happens! and Life Loves You (co-written with Louise Hay).

"If you have embarked on a journey of healing and transformation and seek inspiration, then Memoir of a Mystic by Melissa Amos is sure to stoke your inner fire…"

- Blue Marsden: Hay House Author

"Melissa Amos is a phenomenal teacher and accurate channel who is able to bridge the realms through her many skills as an intuitive and coach, I recommend her skills to anyone who's ready to know themselves on a deeper level."

- Kyle Gray: Speaker, Teacher, Yogi

"Memoirs of a Mystic in Training is an essential read for all those interested in the realm of spiritual exploration. Melissa guides readers through her own personal adventure with spirit, generously sharing her wisdom gained from the trials and tribulations she faced as a mystic in training.

Her remarkable openness and candidness serve as a comforting reminder that we are not alone in our own life journeys. As her captivating story unfolds, I was in awe of all the unfolding synchronicities that weave through her experiences, revealing how Spirit is woven into both the mundane and extraordinary moments of life."

– *Jessica Pashcke: Spiritual Teacher and host of Adventures in Spirit Podcast*

"Melissa Amos is an exquisite Soul of light, who offers deep and heartfelt insight through her experiences, in this beautifully written and totally accessible book If you want to shine bright and find confidence, wisdom and joy, then this book is for you.

The book is outstanding because Melissa is outstanding. My advice: read it, take a deep breath and then begin your own journey with Melissa's guidance. You have everything to gain."

– *Laura Mitchell: Sound Healer, Sound Shaman*

"I could not put this down. As the chapters flow, Melissa's absolute delight and joy in her skills is intoxicating and inspiring in equal measures"

– *Alex Coward: Creator of The Business Freedom Method*

"Being transported into Melissa's world is like going on a journey inside your own soul - you can connect to every single thing she shares as if it happened to you. Such is Melissa's talent in telling a story and keeping you on your toes every step of the way.

Whether it's the characters in the book, her injured (and rather gruesome) foot or the new job she hates, you'll find yourself devouring each word as if your life depends on it.

To me, going through this experience with Melissa felt like climbing a mountain - when we reached the top together, I wasn't the same person I was when I read the first sentence.

As it turns out, sometimes we can't see the big picture of our own life until we read about someone else's and get perspective. "Memoirs of a mystic in training" is about Melissa's life, yet it helped me make sense of my own.

Without revealing too much, let's say once you read this book you might end up inspired to write your own - that's the influence this woman has on so many of us who've followed her journey for years. As you're about to dive in, prepare for the dive to be much deeper, much more profound and a little bit weirder than you expected."

— *Desislava Dobreva: The Branding Queen*

"Memoirs of a Mystic is a truly immersive tale that takes you on many journeys.

Melissa seamlessly weaves together the physical and the seemingly-fantastic, asking many of the same questions I've heard repeated in my own head.

As she untangles the threads of her experience, exploring how everything seems to be connected (and what that might truly mean), you begin to understand the patterns and events in your own life- and what they're really trying to tell you.

Any human who's undertaken (or contemplated) any kind of transformational inner work will find themselves in these pages."

— *CiCi Reagan, Author*

No Matter how far you have come in your journey, or if you re just starting, Memoirs of a Mystic; In Training is the kind of book you would look to for inspiration.

Open, honest and real. Written truly from the heart with energy flowing throughout- like magic

— *Ioanna Schiza: Global Product Developer, Banking*

Preface:

I wasn't sure if this book would ever come about, although looking back I see the inevitability of it. Like so many of us on this planet, we doubt our validity, our experience. We wonder who and what we are, and who we are to share what we know.

Yet here we all are, inevitably doing our best, trying to navigate in any way we know how. Maybe that is through our experience of the 3D world- like who we are in terms of our roles, our jobs, our responsibilities. Perhaps this progresses into something more. Are we the only ones here? Is there more to life than this? Who actually AM I, in the deeper sense of the word?

When the hardships happen, is there a reason, a purpose beyond what is there in the moment? Why do bad things happen to good people, and if there was a God, how could they allow that to be? Is there destiny, or purpose, or do I create the world as the new age would have me believe?

These are all questions I have asked myself. It seems my mind is only happy when contemplating these conundrums. Which led me to asking, *"Why would that be, if I weren't to share it and explore the concepts?"*

Through the hundreds of Soul Explorers I have worked with, I have come to realise something: that we are all journeying through this often crazy world together. That many of us have similar questions, plights, triggers and wonderment.

I also learned that we all have a purpose, and part of mine was to get these words down. To share the questions and the doubts I had. To share with others the answers to the questions that had followed me for so long.

This book takes you through my story, so far. The mystical moments and the magnificent messiness that helped shaped who I became. Yet, as I read the words back for the first time, I realise how many of these words came from somewhere larger than my own.

A sharing of my Soul as my Human navigates through this experience right here in the Human body. With ego, and emotions, and experiences. With the full spectrum of life that we take in through our unique lenses.

This story helps you understand how I made sense of the world. As the words formulated, it helped me too.

As you read this, I hope you feel the transmission of energy as it seeks to expand and soothe you. I hope you invite in the wisdom of your Soul to contemplate the very questions I asked myself, that led me to explore the path less travelled. Perhaps some chapters will help you navigate your journey, acting as a guidebook, rather than a roadmap. Or maybe you will just enjoy as you laugh with (at) me, and how my brain has interpreted life when my Soul was clearly nudging me in other directions.

What I share here is my experience. Sharing teachings from the books, courses and the mentors that I have had the honour of working with along the way. I cannot claim all the ideas as my own, yet everything has been shared from my own unique lens of the world.

So, take what resonates. Question what doesn't. Ask your Soul to guide you through to your truth, and to feed you as you evolve through your journey.

Know this- we are all special and we all have purpose. We have all chosen this very unique time in history to be here, to incarnate on this beautiful Earth. If you have found yourself with this book in your hands, know too that you are indeed also a Mystic in Training. After all, aren't we all in some way?

I hope you enjoy these words.

The Why

I often wonder where it all started. As I look back, I found myself thinking about what I have achieved, where everything has led to, what the actual point is, and I realised something.

It's not the achievements that hold the answer.

The certifications that I worked hard for (or even the ones that came easy).
The recognition from others that I held in such high regards.
The skills I learnt and developed.
The places I travelled, the experiences I had.
The people I met.

It is none of those, and all of those,

One by one, compounding on each other, each step weaving into each other in ways that, *down here,* I couldn't quite comprehend. One action, followed by an incident, that led to this or that. Quite often completely unrelated, sometimes super hard, often as just an occurrence that at the time did not even seem to hold much weight.

But it was all there, a journey.

There was something. Something that wove through the whole experience that I called my life.

From the people I met, from the experiences I had, from the places I travelled. Through the skills I developed and learned. From all of it, but none of it at the same time.

It is as if, looking back, life held a series of opportunities. Opportunities that I could choose- either pick them up or turn the other way. Who knew that each one of them would somehow lead me to where I am now?

A life that I have created; an understanding of myself deeper than I thought possible; an experience of the energetics that underpin the world; and me, there, right there, creating the experiences that push me, support me, and lead me into more. More depth, more breadth, more of life, more of me.

How could I have known? Although perhaps somewhere, some part of me knew all along. As a deeply curious, self-acclaimed geek, and a natural (quantum) physicist with a thirst for the answers to the big questions that most people wouldn't even ask; perhaps it was destined to be,

Whatever it was, this is my story. All of it. How it unfolded, the challenges, the growth, the life affirming parts, and all the bits in between. My hope is you read it and you recognise something in you that is willing to know more, to learn, to grow, to question, to become. For who knows, this very book could be one of *'those'* incidents for you.

It's Got To Start Somewhere

Deep would have been one way to describe me as a kid. My mum always said that growing up I just kinda took things on the chin and didn't seem phased by much (even when my older brother pushed me over when I learned how to sit up, because what kind of two-year-old wants a baby in the house really?). Little did she know that, whilst on the outside I was holding everything together like some serene little swan; on the inside I was regurgitating, unravelling, questioning, imagining, internalising, wondering… No wonder I looked so quiet. I was probably buried down some rabbit hole or another, curious about the inner workings of the universe, even at the ripe young age of five.

I guess this brings me to this natural disposition towards the immaterial world. The invisible realm that resides inside us. The depths that we can journey and travel. The places we can be. The impact we can have. The experiences that go on. They were always so much bigger than what was being seen on the surface. The rest of the world, however, didn't seem to notice. They were all so busy doing their thing, worried about what was going on out there, concerned with everything that was matter.

Did they not see the same things I did?

I was learning fast that it is much more comfortable to project everything outwards than explore within. Stop daydreaming, pay attention, stop wasting time. Just get this done. Think about what you're doing. *Grow up*! This is how we get on in life. We see what is right in front of our noses, and we worry about what might happen. We make lists and we follow the head not the heart.

Life isn't easy, I learned; it is not meant to be. And the only thing that is real is what you can see in front of your face. The rest? Well, the rest is Child's Play.

This message was surrounding me, as this was the world I, like everyone around me, was being trained to live in.

My love of daydreaming. Of making up little stories in my head. Of pretend play. Of spending hours at the bottom of the garden trying to find a four-leaf clover left by a fairy. The hours I spent, lost in books like the Magic Faraway Tree, Matilda, The BFG,- which in many ways felt more real, more comfortable, more alive for me than the reality that I was presented with. This was what we did for *fun*. And being a grown up isn't about fun. That has got to wait for playtime.

Yet, there was one place I knew that my daydreams were accepted. Not just that! Encouraged. A place the whole family would visit every month, yet it was me that was taken aside, and allowed to explore and become. To be myself, and a whole lot more.

The Rainbow Bridge

Visiting my Grandmother was always a joy for me. Our monthly visits would take me to places so far and wide. On hot air balloons, to beautiful, secluded beaches, to rainbow filled landscapes and into a soft cosy corner somewhere there in the depths of my mind.

We visited the centre of a created universe, the highest of the highest heights, and the deepest depths of a beautiful clear ocean, without ever leaving the comfy cosy peach chair that sat in the corner of her warm and welcoming dining room.

How lucky was I, that my grandmother- Molly Ann Smith (lovingly referred to as Molly-Nana or Nana), was a healer. All the way back then, in the 1980's when the closest thing to a local village healer was some joke on the TV, my Nana was a trained Clinical Hypnotherapist, Thought Field Therapist and Neuro-Linguistic Practitioner.

I look back and realise how brave she was. A Jewish woman- who had been brought up in a very traditional home, following her passions. As well as a healer, she was also talented musician, a wonderful pianist who taught children on her own mini grand piano, which took pride of place in her living room. I often wonder what her parents would have thought, the battles she must have had with herself around her beliefs. Her brother a very respected Doctor, her father a businessman, her mother, the vision of the head of a Jewish household. Yet nothing stopped her. She took what she loved and made it work. Wow, she must have helped hundreds, maybe even thousands of people in her lifetime, through her busy local practice. Training with the best in the industry, and doing her work, whilst still attending the local synagogue and playing her role in the community.

How can one not be inspired by that?

For me, I had the biggest treat. My nana, constantly learning new skills and techniques, and me the willing volunteer. Whenever we made the two-hour trip up the motorway, I always hoped she would give me that look, and take me in to that little room, on that comfy peach sofa, and let time slip away.

How did she even know I needed that? I don't even remember there often being a 'thing' that we were working on. An intervention to help heal a symptom. Most often, it was simply there for a pleasure. A time in my life, a few sacred moments every few weeks, where I could explore. Where I could allow my brain to discover, and rest. Where I didn't have to work things out but could come upon what it was that my mind wanted to share with me. A place where imagination was queen, and it led to a sense of calm, acceptance and wild potential.

Something happens I think to a young brain that has the permission to explore worlds beyond what we know. To be shown the power of the mind in real and tangible ways.
Like when I would be sitting there, simply listening to a little story that seemed to bounce and dance around my mind, and she would ask me to gently open my eyes and look at my hand which was hovering weightlessly, held up by nothing but an imaginary-coloured balloon that she had tied around my wrist.

Like when I was scared about how I would perform in exams, or at an event and she had me ground into my current feelings, and then imagine what it was that I really wanted, which we anchored into a Circle of Excellence in front of me, and she would have me step in and embody those feelings of trust.

Perhaps it was those journeys, those moments of bliss, that my little mind used to enjoy every few weeks, that awakened something within me. A fascination of the mind and body connection. An entry into a realm that I couldn't see with my eyes open. A feeling that was available to me just by imagining my Nana saying that magic word... *now*.

Maybe it was that my Nana recognised in me the depth of my mind; the big questions that I asked even when I was 3 or 4. My natural desire to escape the real world and be in my daydream fantasy life. The way I blocked out emotions that were too hard for me to handle. The sensitivity I held as an empathic Soul who naturally took on the weight of the world but acted like nothing had happened. Maybe she saw that, and that was why we journeyed together so frequently. Or maybe my Nana was a gift from God to me, to help me become who I am, and ultimately bring these words to you. After all, it was her who made me promise that one day I would write- as she only weeks before she passed began to do herself.

What I do know is this: that our relationship helped me navigate through what I was becoming. Growing up in that strange era we now call the Xennials, fuelled by change and adaptation. She was there, this constant reassurance that our minds hold such a capability, that we could, in fact, do anything, so long as we believed.

I often wonder if we are brought here to heal something in our lineage, our DNA line, our family history. Perhaps neither of us could have done it without each other. She always said I was a blessing- I am not sure if I ever told her that I thought the exact same of her.

Growing Up

Naturally, life journeys on. Becoming a teenager in a world that was constantly changing and growing. Trying to keep up with the materialistic view that was always so important. The introduction of new technology from a mainly analogue age. My parents divorcing just as I turned 12 and finding my place in a huge new secondary school that I was trying to belong in.

School was, as you can imagine, a trial. I had many friends, yet I was never sure anyone really *got* me. I truly felt that most of the time no one really liked me, and one day they would find out that I wasn't really funny, or clever, or even very nice. Besides, my brain kept taking me round on tangents, on top of trying to juggle the social life of someone who so desperately wanted to fit in, and with an inner rebel who so desperately wanted to shock and stand out, I also had my studies and then the inner geek who just wanted to understand everything.

My school was in central London in one of the hippest, alternative towns in the country. A Jewish School in the middle of Camden Town, we were quite used to standing out amongst the locals as we swarmed in like Smurfs in our little blue uniforms.

Religious education was pretty high up on the agenda. The stories of the past, the practices we were shown, the rituals, the discussions: it was pretty fascinating, and I would find myself journeying along to ancient lands- feeling, seeing, knowing what was happening as the story unfolded. Sometimes it felt like I was part of them.

When the class was ever asked, *"Any questions…?"* it was usually my little hand that went up and asked a little nugget of a question, to which the reply was often one of two things… *"Free Will"* or *"I'll get back to you"* (which by the way, rarely happened).

This left me a little disenchanted. And all the questions were giving me a bit of a reputation amongst the RE department. They probably thought I was being ostentatious, but (*I promise sir*), it was curiosity (*honest*) that started the line of questioning. There were so many questions unanswered, and there was no way my little brain was going to let it go. This was the sort of thing that kept me up at night- especially if I wasn't distracted by all of the goings on of my social life, love life, and all that razzmatazz.

No one could answer me how if billions of people would follow this or that religion, how THIS could be the only one that was right. Or how God might punish me and judge me for a mistake I may have made. Or even how I would have to dedicate my life to the study of a book written thousands of years ago in order to become a Spiritual being, when to me, surely, God was there.

One day, as an intrepid teen, I remember boldly claiming, *"I believe in God, but I don't believe in religion"*.

I wasn't sure really what to do with this information, but there was something deep within me that knew there was more to life than what we see out there. There wasn't really anyone I could ask either. The school were too worried about following the curriculum and keeping us as faithful to the religion as possible (don't even ask what happened when I asked about Jesus), to allow for any meaningful discussion.

My father, an Israeli who had literally fought in wars for his land and beliefs. My mother, the daughter of a converted Jew who had to take her duty very seriously in order to be accepted by the community. And my friends? Well, they didn't really care as we were all too busy being teenagers than to worry about that kind of thing.

So, I suppose I parked it. And allowed for the regular pressures of a regular 15-year-old girl, growing up in London to get the better of me. Yes, I had a bit of a reputation amongst the faculty, but I was bright and despite it all I wanted to do well... so I turned to the only place I could really know and trust to help relieve the buildup that was slowly getting the better of me.

So, where did I turn?

Nana, of course. One day she had me in a trance, commanding that my brain can take in double the amount of information during my revision time- literally helping me expand time. (This is priceless for a busy 15-year-old who just has so much to do). She helped me develop a photographic memory to memorise the facts and figures (which, by the way, got me from achieving a test score of 19% in History in Year 8 to getting an A in my GCSE's- thank you Nana). She helped me visualise myself into success through a little technique called the Circle of Excellence. She also helped keep me calm in exam settings and stressful school moments by setting me an anchor point to use when things got overwhelming.

Was my Nana a part of my success at coping through school? 100%. But there was something else looking back that played an even bigger role. Something that, at the time, was pretty inconsequential to her and for which I had zero idea of what impact this one fateful session would have for me.

I was invited to go to a show to see Paul McKenna - a famous stage hypnotist- and I was so excited because THIS is my idea of entertainment. I went to Nana's all excited that this is going to happen, but straight away she told me that it wasn't a good idea.

"I don't want you clucking like a chicken on stage."

She obviously knew the power of hypnosis and didn't want little influential me being implanted with something I might regret. So, she began to hypnotise me so that I wouldn't be able to be hypnotised by anyone- UNLESS (and here's the clincher) it was for my highest good.

Those were her words.

Unless it is for my highest good, implants, commands, and suggestions would not be taken by me.

"Wow."

She did it to protect me from charlatans (who by now were popping up more frequently). What she actually did in the moment was so powerful that it changed how I interacted with the world for the rest of my life.

Something I discovered many years later…

I mean, have you ever wondered what it is that shapes our opinions, our beliefs, our theories of life?

We are always being bombarded with information. We are constantly being given hidden messages by the world, the media, advertising and even the people around us. Of course, the marketers of the world know this all too well.

But suddenly, they didn't seem to work on me quite so effectively. Suddenly the propaganda machine didn't seem to hit me like it did before. Suddenly, I seemed happier to walk the road less travelled because I wasn't quite so impressionable by the subliminal…

Perhaps, perhaps it was the 16-year-old me that was the catalyst to me breaking free from the Matrix- before I even knew it was there.

I appreciate this all sounds a little magical. Maybe you're even thinking, I wish I had that implanted in my head when I was younger too… but it should come with a warning.

Teenagers tend to gravitate towards those that have the same beliefs and interests as themselves. Sometimes, I felt so out of the loop because I didn't buy in to the latest craze, or weird tasting drink. My music taste was eclectic to say the least (you would often find me at the local heavy metal gig, yet equally as comfortable in the jazz cafe).

Couple that with being super sensitive, just 'knowing' when people were talking about you, or feeling uncomfortable around you, and triple that with the deep thinker that had a great capacity of making up stories- it often led me to feeling quite alone and confused- even when I was surrounded by people.

Now, of course I realise the gift it was. Back in teenage land… maybe not so much. Yet maybe somehow this was all part of something much bigger.

The Divine Matrix

There is a power that is greater than us. Something out there that is influencing our thoughts, our actions, our dreams, and our desires. Yet we don't always consider what that might be.

We hear, *the universe has your back,* that we are supported by this force that is constantly working in our favour and won't let us fail. To trust in the powers that be, and surrender to it, because there's no way it will let us fail. Destiny will lead us somewhere and it's written in the stars.

On the other hand, we hear that the world is out to get you, not to trust the powers that be. That the world is run on magic, and with AI and big brother, and subliminal messages that we are being manipulated into a life that is disempowered and reliant upon 'the system'. Pair that with the belief that our thoughts are literally creating everything (and sometimes, most of the time our thoughts seem destructive), and then we might be left bumbling around, wondering what, who and if indeed there is anything we can actually trust.

I have my own conclusions, which I have drawn through looking back upon my life and noticing some patterns. That there is for sure 'something' that is influencing us, and having an awareness of that makes all the difference. But it is more than this. Through our path we can decide- who or what are we tapping into, and who or what is making the decisions or the circumstances that we find ourselves in.

I mean, have you ever really thought about it? If our thoughts create our things, what is it that creates our thoughts? If we are surrendering to something, what is it that we are surrendering to? If we are asking for guidance from something bigger than us, who or what has the wisdom to give us that advice, and is it really aligned to our highest good?

Are we really in control? Are things truly destined? Could my astral chart, my Bezi chart, my Human Design, my Soul Plan, my Religion, my Ancestral line, my Akashic Records, my beliefs, my personality type, my *anything* truly be the answer? If so, which one is 'right' and what is really the point of it all? Are we trying to break free from a Matrix that isn't serving us, or is there something else that is just there if we just tap into it? And how do we do that if it's true? Is divinity out there or in here? And where, oh where, do these answers lie?

Perhaps the answer is actually all of it. Where your attention flows energy goes. Perhaps there is a grand plan, and the *free will* that my RE teacher answered me for every single question I asked; is, indeed, the answer. Perhaps it is that there are a number of matrix systems out there; those aligned to our highest greatness, our Soul's destiny, our purpose if you like, and those that are here to distract us. To keep us powerless and confused and bumbling around like a fly trying to escape through a closed window.

What if that is where our free will is trying to make the best choices; by aligning to a divinity in this web we find ourselves in. Maybe, in fact all is true, and it's up to us to figure out which one we choose.

In case you're wondering, yes, this little paragraph is exactly where my head goes when you give me some quiet time- welcome to my brain.

Free Will, Or Destiny?

Life seems to just happen, somehow unfolding, decision by decision, moment by moment. The school days, the college where I thought I would tackle Biology and Chemistry because I knew even at 16. I wanted to help people. I was also inspired by my uncle, Ami, who is an Osteopath. Having had back issues myself, I wanted to help others resolve and heal.

I saw this glamorous life with my own studio and clients where I could do just that. Besides, Science was my favourite subject in school.

How was I to know that I picked two of the most yawn subjects? Turns out I am a physicist not a chemist but thank the days I had my Psychology A level to enjoy twice a week! I was increasingly getting a great feeling that this was not the way I wanted to spend my heady college years and, much to the delight*(!)* of my parents, I quit the Sciences and switched to Business Studies.

Hallelujah! I found something fun, useful and somewhere I could apply this thing I knew I wanted- to make a difference somehow in the world. But would I ever know how this all fit together?

My days at university were interesting, and it was then I found my voice. University wasn't really how I imagined it. You were left very much to your own devices- attending lectures, doing coursework, working independently or in small groups. The-

gasp- presentations seemed to be incessant. It felt as though every week we had to present on something.

Now, public speaking wasn't really my thing. I counted myself as an introverted extrovert (or maybe the other way around). I was in my head a lot of the time, worried what people would think of me, judging others and how they showed up, wanting to fit in, but wanting to not be a part of the crowd- indie rock chick FYI; it was certainly daunting. I was right there, in my life, and I felt so grown up (18, at university, with a car, a job, a mobile phone and a local pub!), I probably had a lot to prove and not much life experience to back it up.

Yet, something happened on one of those very first classes.

In my head there were at least 100 people in that class- but realistically, it was probably more like 40. We had to stand up and do a presentation on (wait for it) the third generation of phones! The future thinking me had already had the idea that wouldn't it be handy to have your whole music library on your phone (Apple missed a trick with me). In the days before Google was really a thing, my technological know-how was pretty low on my agenda.

Anyway, I am there, sitting with these nerves in my belly, feeling like my root chakra is about to fall out of my pants, thinking,
"OMG, what am I going to say? I don't know what I am doing, they're all gonna laugh at me, there's a fit guy in the corner and I definitely haven't been here long enough to establish myself." I looked around and came to the conclusion that I didn't fit in. I looked like the weirdo, and I was definitely going to mess this up.

But, as I sat there and heard student after student presenting their view, mumbling, fumbling, talking down at the lectern (I didn't even know it was called a lectern), and generally just hoping the ground would swallow them up, I decided something.

Maybe, maybe... if I just *looked* like I knew what I was doing... Maybe if I just spoke out to the room and pretended I wasn't about to run and drop out my insides... Maybe if I just shared the ideas I had and hoped for the best... Maybe I would do ok...

So, I said a little prayer-

"Thank you, whoever you are for not making me look like a fool and giving me at least a bit of street cred."- and I got up there.

I looked to the very back of the room and started speaking. I even made eye contact (briefly) with the teacher. I am pretty sure I even smiled at some point. I pretended I was confident; a part of me believed that too. Before I knew it, my 3 minutes were over, and I sat down with the knowledge that something had happened to me in that time.

Who knew that would be such a turning point?

I had spoken and no one threw rotten tomatoes at me. I survived, and more than that, I inspired somebody. My classmates asked me, *"How did you do it?"* I shrugged. I thought about my 'circle of excellence' that my Nana had taken me through. I did it. And now everyone wanted me to be in their group because I- shy me who thought everyone hated her- could nail a presentation. *I hoped they didn't find out how I was **really** feeling.*

That night I thought to myself, *"Wow! How's that as a power to create a new identity?"*

I proved something to myself. Something left me in that moment.

I knew I would learn something at university, but I couldn't imagine it would have been that.

I figured I would be learning academia to help me move through my life and make me be this high-flying success that seemed so farfetched from where I was in that moment. Maybe, this was the circle of excellence in action. Feeling what I was feeling in the moment, deciding how it is I would rather feel, and then quite literally stepping into that place and allowing it to be true. Perhaps, I was learning that I could do something, even if I thought I couldn't. Maybe there were untapped resources in me that were just waiting to be, well tapped.

How would I ever find them? I wasn't sure I believed in me, let alone anyone else. It seemed to me, however, that everyone was so wrapped up in their own selves, that maybe I could try things after all, and they might not be so dangerous.

Do I fake it? Try it on for size? Envision, wonder?

Fake It Till You Make It

Is that even a thing?

Isn't this path about being authentic, being the true you? So how can faking it change anything? Isn't that just being disingenuous?

Yet I wonder. Perhaps it is not the fear of doing something that is the truth. Perhaps that is what we are faking because we have picked up evidence of it through the past, through our lens of the world, through our peers and our experience.

Maybe it's not faking it; maybe it's trying something on. Trying on a different mask or a different way of doing things.

Maybe it's the way that we show up, having been moulded through the years by our parents, our caregivers, our teachers, our peers, our society, our community, our television shows, and our expectations. Maybe it's *that* that is the lie. When we feel that rumble in our belly, it's a part of us that is untapped; a reminder of who we truly are that is wanting to be unleashed.

Maybe we aren't faking it. Maybe we are just breaking through something that we just accepted as fact. But it wasn't. It never was.

And maybe, maybe, our greatest fear is actually our biggest gift waiting to be realised. Maybe it's our path to find the resources to break through it.

If that is by hoping, praying, leaping and wishing for the very best- despite our insides flipping around like a scene out of *Cirque du Soleil,* maybe there's something in it about playing our part, which is actually us realising ourselves and who we are truly becoming.

I have certainly had experience where I have just found myself doing things. Unsure what or how I will manage. Feeling completely ill prepared (despite how much I have, indeed, prepared). My physical body seemingly leading me into a situation and as I arrive there, take that stand, take centre stage, in that very moment, a huge leap occurs. Would it have occurred without it? Perhaps, somehow. Or maybe we are delaying the inevitable. Had I had done what I expected in that fateful moment at the University lectern, would I have, in that moment, sealed my fate as a shy, mumbling, stumbling bumblebee?

It's kind of like parenthood. Until you're in it, how could you ever know how, what, where, who; yet you do it, and suddenly, you are the parent. It couldn't have happened any other way.

Maybe that lesson is to trust ourselves more.

Right?

Perhaps It's In The Quantum

Wanna know something I learned recently? In the mystical and magical world of quantum physics- something doesn't manifest or occur until there's an observation of it.

In the famous double split experiment (where a light was observed as both a particle and a wave, depending on what the experimenter was looking for), it showed that a thing isn't a thing until it was known to be a thing! And even then, it can be a different thing depending on what we expect... (*want to know more? Check out Thomas Youngs original experiment from 1801*).

Now, isn't that interesting?

That we have a potential- a series of probabilities and possibilities that are right there in the thought we are about to action, or the word we are about to speak. Depending on how we approach it and how we observe it, will depend on whether it will go this way or that... whether it will become the particle or the wave... whether it will become the celebration or the failure.

Depending on what we expect.

I wonder as we begin to look at our life with this knowing- as we journey together through my experience in these words- if we begin to see this.

Of course, life does bring its surprises, its miracles and its curveballs. As we adventure on, let's discover together what this means for us as we live this great life we have been gifted.

It makes me wonder. Have you ever had an incident where you were so sure of something; The colour of a painting, a saying on the wall, the name of a favourite dish, what happened in movie, which, not until it is discussed with a friend do you realise that you may have simply fabricated those details? Now you've seen it 'their' way, there's no going back. Of course, it was like that all along, *wasn't it?*

How many of our memories are truly true? How much of my life as I knew it to be was actually factually correct? Was it all just a figment of my imagination? Did I speak it all in to being? Who or what is it that fundamentally decides that yes, that wall is blue, despite me seeing it as grey my whole life. Is anyone right? Or Wrong? How much of my story is actually My Story, and how much His-Story?

All I know is what I know, or at least what I think I know. All I can share through these words is the journey. From my perspective. Through my beliefs. Willing to be open enough to know, that truth has, indeed, a thousand perspectives.

It does make me wonder. What is it about my story that found me in the family, the circumstances and the situation I was in, growing up in the leafy suburbs of greater London?

The Power Of Word

What was it that saw me born into the family I did, I wondered. I was born to an Israeli father, who had fought in wars, and an English mother, granddaughter of a converted Jew, whose heritage was from Eastern Europe- holocaust survivors.

Both my grandmothers were extraordinary women. My paternal grandmother had travelled miles from her home in Aden, with 12 children, to move to the promised land in Israel. My maternal grandmother was a musician, healer and divorcee who had created the life that she wanted, going against the grain of what was expected.

From a young age, I learned Hebrew- how to read and write it. I thought the letters of this different alphabet were fascinating. When family came over, I used to listen, mesmerised by the sounds so unfamiliar to my native ears, without understanding the words but feeling their impact. My prayers as a child were often regurgitated in Hebrew from what I had learned in school. Whilst I could only speak it slightly and had a surface understanding which just about got me by during my numerous holidays to the beautiful land of Israel, it took me many years to understand how significant this exposure would be.

Hebrew is an ancient language; one of the originals. According to Jewish Mysticism, the word is what creates. That there is no separation from the word to the manifestation.

Indeed, you can look at the numerology and the meaning of many Hebrew words and understand that one does not just label something- it creates the building blocks of the very thing it is describing (you can find out more- start with the word for circumference in Hebrew which can be calculated to 3.1415)

Things were just about starting to get fascinating here…

It was during a journey in my reiki training that I was reminded of my connection to my Hebrew origins, when I was invited to discover my Book of Life and I saw my Hebrew name– Manucha- printed in Hebrew lettering on the cover. This name means rest, calm, and serenity. Upon connecting in this way, seeing it in my mind's eye etched on this huge book, it was as if this serenity was beginning to wash over me. A feeling I hadn't experienced in a long time. Quite different, may I add, to the teasing from my brother that my Hebrew name translated to 'lazy', which I had internalised and believed for a long, long while. I wonder for that to be another dichotomy that has been so prevalent in my life as my English name, Melissa translates as honeybee, who are notorious for their busy-ness. (And there's a story for another time).

Some years later, the language found me again.

A series of coincidences and opportunities came to me when I found myself on a course with zero idea of what to expect. On the first day when the course creator, Blue Marsden, started to speak of the 22 letters of the Hebrew Alphabet, of the Sefer Yitzeret and of the symbols that accompanied them, my whole body stood on end. *I was in the right place.*

Our name and the way our letters correspond to this ancient language came together with a meaning. Creating the building blocks of our journey, our Soul's destiny- the talents, the challenges and the goals that we faced and moved through in the course of this incarnation. It made such sense to me. First, we are word!

The letters and the numbers bounced off the page as we began to learn the meanings. It was a deep remembering of something that must have uncovered in me long ago.

My Soul Plan was awakened, and now I had the means to help others discover their blueprint too. I understood those dichotomies that were so present in my every day. The need for freedom, the thirst for learning. The quest to search for all the answers from outside of me and the reluctance to seek within. Somehow, this system seemed to compliment, and add depth to what I knew of my Astrology chart, and later on, my Human Design. My name, which my mum had shared with me changed the moment I was born as I didn't look like a 'Deborah', held the energies that were influencing me through my life.

Oh, how I contemplated what this meant. What came first, the me who then had a name and so took on these traits, or was this all some divine plan, to help us to incarnate into just the right circumstances, to help us grow and achieve this destiny that we had found in ourselves?

I knew this- another series of events and circumstances led me to utilising something that I hadn't considered to be significant, until it became so.

This Soul Plan of mine was working all along, and somehow, understanding this blueprint helped me to understand myself better! I wasn't lazy, I was serene. I wasn't nosy, I was curious. I wasn't morbid, considering as I did about the afterlife- I was following my Soul Destiny. Along the way, I had picked up coping mechanisms, habits, understandings, beliefs to help me muddle through with all that I was dealing with. Yet it was leading to something so much more.

And then there was another discovery.

You see, the sciences fascinated me, along with my depth of curiosity of the way the world works. My growing desire to learn more and more, and my thirst for expansion, led me to start to delve into metaphysics.

One weekend in 2022, I found myself in a conference filled with the most fascinating of speakers combining Spirituality, Ancient Mysticism with Science and Metaphysics. During a talk by the one and only Gregg Braden, he began to present about the origins of the human. The coding we all have within. The texts which state that first there was the word. That the true essence of us is written. As he began to explain the genetic make-up of us humans, the building blocks of what makes us who we are, I saw it all fall into place.

This is why I studied year one of Biology- to understand Genetics.
This is why I learned to read Hebrew- to extract meaning from these letters right now.
This is why I recited the Hebrew prayers as a child- to remember.

As Gregg stated in his alluring voice, it means one thing…

"God Eternal Within Body- YHVH "

Every single one of the hairs on my body stood on edge.

This is IT!
We ARE eternal beings.

We ARE here for purpose.
We ARE coded for greatness.
The answers ARE all lying here within.

Somehow, through these seemingly random learnings, skills and talents, I was sitting right there in the middle of a conference hall in London, with this Ancient Knowledge which is now satisfied by my science brain.

The connections and the neurones were firing like crazy. I was seeing the link between these and the sacred sounds. I was understanding all I was reading from other works of Paul Selig *(I Am Word)*. The Akashic Records suddenly made a lot more sense, and living the Soul Led Life became more alive. The reason for stillness exemplified, the search for answers satisfied and opening to a whole new level.

For a moment, it all finally made sense.

Maybe nothing is random at all.

The Next Step

Who knew a BA (Hons) in Business Studies would lead me to where I was going next? Through my college days, I always loved cars and developed a very useless skill of being able to identify almost any car just by its headlight (IKR?). In fact, my school yearbook had my likely job as owning my own motorbike shop (not sure). To help pay my way through University, I found myself working in a car showroom, answering phones and booking cars in.

I don't know what it was about me, but I was seen as way more capable than I actually was. Age 18 and so shy inside, I was left at one point having to manage 7 technicians, allocate their jobs and manage a workshop. Never mind I had only been driving a few months, didn't know my way around a car (yes, I could ID a headlight, but a head gasket? No idea). But I soon found my voice; I had to. Customers shouting at me, technicians not listening to me, bosses just expecting me to know what I was doing. Overwhelmed is an understatement. Somehow, I survived.

I worked my way across and up quite quickly, working at 4 of the busy sites in the area. This was where I met my future husband Mark, who was selling cars at one of the smaller sites in the group.

When I graduated in the summer, I had some grand plans for myself. Armed with a degree and a boyfriend, I fancied more than whatever *this* seemed to be bringing me (by the way, so much- confidence, a work ethic, belief in myself, a way to handle myself around men, technical knowledge of cars, sexism and mild harassment) we quit our jobs and went travelling around the world.

This. Is. The. Life.

No one to answer to. Nowhere to be, apart from the next stop on the trip. No work. No homework. No parents. No worries.

Apart from one little hitch…

A week before the trip of a lifetime, I got a call from my mum.

"Is your foot, OK? There's been a few cases of a nasty foot infection at the gym."
"Nope, I'm ok", I said.

Next day, itchy toe. I tried to ignore it, but it got worse. With 4 days to go, I headed to the doctor who prescribed something to help. 24 hours later, my foot looked like something out of a horror movie, I couldn't put any pressure on it, and every minute the swelling seemed to double in size.

Uh oh.

One trip to A&E later and the words, *"Miss, I don't think you'll be going anywhere…"*

But I knew better, and I can be quite stubborn when I want to be.

So, whilst I was meant to be packing, going to visit my friends and family and generally prepping for 3 months of bliss, I was at my mum's, foot elevated, and willing myself to heal.

My parents had been divorced for nearly ten years at this point and had not said more than about 3 words to each other since.

But, if my dad wanted to see me before I went away (which he most definitely did), he would have to come over to my mum's and do so. And he did! And he didn't die or become cursed or whatever it was we all thought would happen. I genuinely think this was the start of more than just healing for my foot.

Maybe this was the start of us all moving forward- whilst I had to be the most still I had been for a long time.

12 hours before the flight, I got the OK to go. Prescribed with crutches, antibiotics and strict instructions from my mum to call her with updates regularly and to be careful, we were on our way!

The delight when we got to London Heathrow, and we were whizzed around by the airport buggy (I always wanted to go on one of those) and then upgraded for our first flight to Toronto! We were there!!! I couldn't walk, but we had made it!

Turned out that crutches + jet lag + antibiotics isn't much fun. Our hotel took one look at me and sourced me a wheelchair.

Being pushed around for 3 days in a busy city really did help me see the world in a different way. People treated you differently.

For those 3 days, there were times where I was subhuman.
For those 3 days, there were times where I was patronised.
For those 3 days there were also times where I found out about the kindness of strangers.

And the importance of a sense of humour.

Like when we crossed a road, hit a curb and I went flying out the wheelchair (the look on the drivers faces, who were queueing at the lights, was pretty priceless). Or when we found ourselves at the top of the steepest staircase with no other way to access the building, and a man offered to carry me down! (I walked, much to his relief). Or the time when A lister Michael Douglas was outside the hotel filming, and because of my apparent disabled status, I was the only person in the crowd he came to say hello to and allowed a picture with.

From down there… a different perspective arose.

It was on our next very long flight to Fiji that things took a turn. Something happened over the international dateline that made my foot swell, and it became reminiscent of Freddy Kruger. I arrived weak and tired with 3 bubbles on my foot that made me wonder whether this was a good idea at all.

We were lucky, for the onsite doctor was there that day. I thought he might grimace when I took off that awful flight sock, but he was completely non-plussed. He took a look and gave me the simplest prescription- go in the sea, every day, 3 times for 3 days.

"That's it?"
'The sea knows how to heal you', he told me. *'Let it clean you, this will go.'*

And so that was what we did.

When I couldn't walk to the sea's edge, the wheelchair couldn't be pushed along the beautiful white sand (yes, we tried) and I was too weak to walk, my boyfriend, Mark, who had spent the last week pushing me around the streets of Toronto, went and found solutions for me. He never once complained that we couldn't see more of this beautiful island we were on, and instead spent the time bathing my feet in fresh sea water and finding creative ways to get around the resort.

3 days later, I saw the doctor again. He was very pleased with how things were progressing. This was not what I saw, which were huge septic bubbles, but okay, he's the pro. He then proceeded to take 3 syringes full of fluid from my ankle and said once again to keep cleaning it in water and it would get better.

And it did! Now I could walk! I must have been asked 7465859 times if I had scraped my foot on the coral, with the cocked heads of the other guests who all gawped at my strange looking foot every time I was wheeled round the resort, but finally I could get my toes in that beautiful sand and was on my way to feeling better.

I am pretty sure this doctor was sent from somewhere for me. In fact, I don't ever remember getting a bill or making a claim on insurance. He showed me that with faith, the elements and a little intervention, the body will do exactly what it needs to do to heal.

Note, Taken.

Next stop, New Zealand, Australia and then to the Far East countries of Malaysia, Singapore and Thailand.

Had this whole thing been manifested? From my mum planting the idea that this horror of a foot infection was bound to have found me, to the will power of my young mind determined that I WILL be on that flight (even the upgrade I had dreamed of), to that doctor who prescribed me only sea water and a specific length of time… that I had healed, somehow. Did my mind have something to do with this? What part did it play? If I had been told something different and fell into victimhood what would have happened, then?

Was this magic? A Placebo? A natural coincidence? Fate?

The Placebo

The placebo effect has always fascinated me. I remember learning about it in science, and I am supposing with my background of the hypnotherapeutic interventions I had experienced so young, I often wondered if it was in fact the idea of something rather than the thing of something that made a thing happen. I had spent my upper teenage life at the birthplace of this very saying. '*If you think you can, or you think you can't, you're probably right*'. (*Henry Ford circa 1947*)

In fact, there have been studies which have shown that drugs of the same ingredients can be 25% more effective if you buy the branded (and more expensive) version, just because we believe that if we pay more for something it will work better. Further studies have shown that we can influence our own immune response by imagining it better, or by simply being told that a technique will help it. (*Dr David Hamilton being a huge influence on my understanding with his very accessible, and often humorous teachings*).

Now, if we can only believe more in the power of our healing and our wellness than in the power of our illness and our disease, perhaps this is the source of our experience. Maybe we are not so powerless after all.

Was it knowing that my foot would take 3 days to heal that meant that miraculously on day 3 I could walk again? Or was the doctor tapping into a knowledge that he knew that that is how long this type of infection takes to go through one's body?

Is this why the zit always appeared when you were stressing about looking good? Was this why luck seemed to find me because I always stated I was lucky? Was it that my superstitions (nope, I don't walk under ladders or put umbrellas up indoors) pay off because I believed them to?

Turns out the science agrees. The brain does not know what is real and what is imagined. Our brain fires off the same responses, and it can even change our muscle mass by thinking we are doing exercise (note to self, as I now think about doing sit ups!). And it has a name- Neuro-plasticity. We can literally train our brain to create pathways of belief. And what you tell the brain to do, the brain will do.

Now, it is not always as simple as that, of course, which is a good thing really. I mean, imagine if every time we had a thought it created that exact manifestation. We would never know if we were coming or going! But it is our dominant thought that will prevail. When it comes to illness and dis-ease, I can think back to the countless times when I had thought myself ill, where the thing didn't hurt until I saw it, and where I had made a miraculous recovery just in time for the weekend. Perhaps the answer is in knowing that the body has full capability to heal. Perhaps focusing on the miracles that occur in our world every day will help our brain to know just how possible our wellness is. Maybe we don't just play victim to our circumstance. Maybe we have the potential inside of us that is greater than what we have ever known.

The power it seems lies within us. And that is an exciting discovery.

The Power lies within us?

Imagine that! No, I mean it. *Truly* imagine it. That your wellness, your vitality, the effectiveness of the medicines you take, or the food you eat are directly affected- improved or reduced by what we believe. Imagine that every time food entered your mouth, you knew it was filled with such love, and blessings and health promoting benefits that your body couldn't help but respond positively to it. Rather than just 'knowing' that the cake will make you gain 10lbs just by looking at it.

What if we knew that when we got a cold, or a bug, our body was naturally doing the best it could to clean us out and return us to health. That this wasn't here to debilitate us, but to provide us rest. And that listening to the mantra, or sipping the broth, or the warm herbal tea is supporting our wellness journey.

Imagine if we knew, truly, that the power of our body was in our minds, and our emotions, and our hands. What would we do differently. How differently would we treat ourselves, speak with ourselves, love ourselves, if we knew that?

Is the Placebo something we should just dismiss as irrelevant, or something we could utilise for the benefit of all?

The Mountain Or The Molehill

The next challenge was just round the corner- as they often are. Travelling around the beautiful lands of New Zealand with a map and no plan in a 2 birth Mercedes Campervan, we just went where our nose took us. Often letting our gut decide when we were driving down a motorway, of whether to go left or right.

I'm not sure if it is just that New Zealand is so jaw droopingly beautiful, yet everywhere we did end up was spectacular. Like we were being led to just the right place. One evening when I called my mum, her friend was round and said,

"Have you gone to that place that smells funny?"
"No", we said, looking at each other like, why would we?

But it turns out that's exactly where we headed the next day. We didn't realise until we both looked suspiciously at each other and wondered what the source of that eggy sulphur smell was!

Rotorua was a beautiful little space, where we experienced live volcanic activity and geysers bubbling out of the ground! Also, a place, it turns out, that is perfect for restoring health and healing the skin, which we took full advantage of with the healing wounds of my foot.

One evening we pulled up in our camper-van at a campsite in the dark. Awakening the following morning to the most picturesque view of a snow-capped mountain in the Southern Island, Mark decided he wanted to go up the mountain.

I didn't really fancy myself as a hiker mountaineer. Besides having just recovered from 2 weeks of not being able to walk, and just about getting my strength back, I apprehensively agreed.

Naive, I think the word is.

The helicopter lifted us up into the beautiful blue skies, so we were looking down on this crisp white untouched mountain. Snow suits and boots on, we landed and the small team of hikers including me (apparently, I am a hiker now), dismounted the craft onto this virgin sand.

It was breath-taking. The views. The air. The cleanliness. The silence descending upon us as the helicopter- our only connection with the civilised world- disappeared out of view. We were left, alone. 5 of us and our young, long haired, long legged male guide.

We walked. I was terrified. Shifting between awe of this serene picture book environment, and the terror of being stranded here for eternity, I think I was in denial for much of the trip. Up and down, over and under, crunching the soft snow beneath our feet. Seeing for miles, a sea of pure brilliant white expanding for eternity.

Until we got to one crevice, and I froze. The guide with his long legs, Mark with his long legs, and everyone else who was clearly more capable than I was, jumped (JUMPED) over this gap which our guide had casually told us was a sheer drop through the mountain.

Errrrrr...

I cannot go any further.

There's no way I'll make it. I am definitely gonna fall and die or get stuck. I was literally and figuratively frozen.
No one else could do it for me, and my feet would not move off the floor.

Now logically, I knew that I couldn't stay where I was, or I would definitely freeze and die. But I also really couldn't get my head around the possibility that my little legs could make it, plus I had little trust in my snow boots to grip to the side, despite it being okay when I was on seemingly solid ground.

Everyone was cheering me on. I was in my head, calculating all the things that can and almost definitely will go wrong. Until something came over me. Something from deep within told me, I will be OK. Something told me-

"Melissa, if you take this leap, everything else will seem easier. Today is not the day you're going to die".

So, I took what I knew. If the sea can heal my foot, and the whole rest of the team can make it through, I can be okay too. I saw it, in my mind, I saw me taking a step. I felt the snow boot solidly gripping to the side wall. I trusted the hand that had reached out to take hold when I was close enough. I visualised the triumphant me on the other side celebrating that I had made it.

I leapt, I gripped, and I kept on moving. Within a moment, Mark's hand was solidly in mine, and I was back to relative safety.
We survived- and now I was ready for MORE!

Of course, this is where the helicopter arrived to take us home. Now that I had developed the trust in myself and my equipment, the whole ordeal was over. I left there with a knowing that if I can do *that,* maybe I had some more surprises up my sleeve.

One thing I have learned as I have moved through this life is that we are way more capable than we think. It is often the thing that we are most scared of that leads to our greatest achievement. It is as if there's a part of us that is more afraid of doing the thing and it changes us, than of doing the thing and getting it wrong. I mean, sure. Getting a leap over a mountain crevice wrong might not just be life changing but life ending, but I mean in the rest of life,. Sometimes the more mundane aspects that makes our stomach leap and our hands shake are just as important. If we can somehow muster up the courage to move from the fear consuming us all to a bravery and a trust in something, the real growth lies just there.

Life wasn't meant to be lived in our comfort zone. The real adventures live just outside it.

Travelling the world and being so far from all that was familiar really helped me to grow up. I was 21 and thinking I knew it all, but I had never lived outside of home. Whilst I was an independent girl- having to travel from the age of 11 into London on the tube for 45 minutes to get to school, socialising in Camden, and having odd jobs since the age of 16 did foster this self-resilience- I was living in this life of routine. Having to be here, do that, start then, finish then. Now I had the ultimate freedom. Apart from the few flights we had booked in-between destinations, the world was literally ours.

Looking back, of course I would have made more of the opportunity. But I was pretty shy and English, which meant we didn't hang out with many of the locals; we mainly kept ourselves to ourselves. But it did mean that Mark and I bonded in a way that was deeper than we could ever have done if we were still in the rat race at home. We ate the local delicacies, we saw the sites that were famous in the area, we lived in caravan sites and even did some camping (once under the watchful eye of an emu, which towered over my short frame). We were carefree and open to life. We let our dreams guide us, and in those 3 months, life was all ours for the taking.

Finally, we returned home. I, of course, had grand plans of where my degree and life experience were going to take me, so I did what every other sensible citizen would do. I found a job.

The Secret Life Of A Car Salesperson

I am not entirely sure that *this* is where I thought I would end up. I found myself working at a prestige car showroom that looked from the outside like a palace, but the story inside was far from ideal.

It wasn't called this, but basically, I worked in the complaints department. I thought those days were behind me, but it turns out the more expensive the car, the more intolerant the customers. I'd come home at night shaking after my 9-hour days of thanklessly appeasing people. Too tired to do anything apart from eat my dinner way too late at night, slump in front of the TV and look forward to my weekends off- which were mainly spent either partying too hard or furnishing our new house. I soon got back into what was expected of me.

Surely there's got to be more than this?

I was frustrated that I wasn't given more responsibility. Frustrated that things were thrust upon me because I was capable and experienced.
Frustrated that I actually cared about the customers and no one else seemed bothered.
Frustrated that I was looking down at the most beautiful cars in the world and I didn't even get to sit in one, let alone drive them.

But I learned and I grew. There's something about the resilience you gain whilst working in the motor trade. We worked hard and we played hard. The banter was relentless, and I homed in on my witty comments and smart-arse comebacks so much that I became the self-appointed *Queen of Puns*.

It made me think on my feet. It built compassion for others without always taking it too personally. I built friendships with the other girls in my team who were all on my side. I had found my people.

Turns out, I was also building a belief that work life was hard. 'The public' were disenchanting me. I would go home at night with those quite dangerous thoughts.

"Is *this all there is? Is this all I am good at? How many of life's problems cannot be resolved?" (*The clincher was when someone's seatbelt feeder (*did you even know that was a thing?*) didn't work on his convertible car and he made such a stink about it, I pretty much gave up on humanity).

Having to get up to do something day in and day out that was just, well, hard. Everyone so busy doing their own thing and trying to keep their own head above water, that no one really cared about what I was doing, unless I was doing it wrong. The customer is always right… (no), which by default meant I was always wrong. My naturally optimistic outlook on life was being severely tested and there were days that I would contemplate my brakes failing, just so I could get some unadulterated time off.

I didn't know it then. Then I thought it was simply how life was built. We work for someone else; we get paid, we go back home, live for the holidays and the weekends and then start again. No, I didn't know it then, but I see it so clearly now. That discomfort I felt. That deep sense of dissatisfaction, of anguish and even the despondency was not just a symptom of life. It was a symptom of living a life that was not true to me. A symptom of living a life that was so far removed from my truth that my Soul was trying to reach out and get my attention.

I clearly didn't listen when I had the freedom of travel. When I saw how life *could* be. When the money was spent and the sun had set, I had gone right back home, right back into the industry that I had sworn myself out of. I was searching for something, but I didn't know what.

The adrenalin hits, the cortisol bursts, the drama… there was something addictive about it, I suppose. How can we know what we don't know? How could I find a way out of this if this is just what life expects of us? After all, there are so many people worse off than me and I should be grateful (and I was at times), but the thought of never getting off this hamster wheel was leaving me disillusioned with life. Something had to change.

So, I looked in the only place I could down.

From my office overlooking the showroom, I would often look down after a pretty angry phone call and think about the salespeople, *"They're in the right place. They drive the cars, they chat to happy customers, they play the game, and they are where the moolah is."*

From where I was sitting, this was the life of glam. It also helped that my now fiancé was a car salesperson and an absolute natural at it that I knew something had to be done.

So, we made it happen!

Within a year, we had established a graduate trainee program, and I had my first company car! I was in my element! Nice cars, great pay, no more, *"Good morning, how can I take your complaint today?"* (Joke). I had found what I thought I was looking for!

What fascinated me the most was the training we got. The sales skills were reminding me of the NLP practices that my Nana had taught me in the past. I was always the first to volunteer for the training courses, which made the rest of the team happy because I was filling the company's quota!

One such time I remember discussing what it is we really do. The trainer said to us all,

"It's not cars you sell, it's something else. Tell me what you do without using car at all."
"I help make people's dreams come true", I said.

As I said it, it felt so right. I am not spending my life hitting targets and making money, I am literally making it possible for someone to drive around in the cars of their dreams.

And that changed everything.

My colleagues couldn't understand my process. It wasn't the same as the 10 other salesMEN in the showroom. I spent time. I knew the name of their cats and children. I understood what made them tick. I spoke to them with a genuine desire to help them get what it was that they wanted. We built relationships. And they bought cars. I wasn't spending time negotiating, I was spending time helping.

Apparently, I made it look easy.

But it wasn't.

The truth was, I was working 50+ hours a week with one weekend off in six. I was under consistent pressure. It didn't matter how good your last month was, on the 1st day of the next one, the board was wiped clean, and your target was set again.

The other departments were not always so open to helping the sales team (because we were the ones who had it easy, right?), so there was a constant battle in getting things done. There were the technical difficulties. There was the sexism that was constantly there. There was the,

*"Hello, can I speak to a sales**man**, please?'* to which I replied, *"Will a saleswoman do?"*

There was the admin. There were the expectations. And it was relentless. I was fuelled on coffee, Diet Coke and quick bites to eat under my desk. Dinner was never before 8pm and was usually a carb fuelled nightmare, before I fell into bed for sleep for an early start again the next day.

Doors slammed in my face if I was 1 minute late (despite still being there an hour after my shift ended). Mystery shoppers came in ALWAYS to me, which were then played on the big screen in front of the whole department and every single word picked apart, criticised, with little regard of little me dying in the corner watching myself at work in front of all my friends, my managers and colleagues. Customer satisfaction surveys were the bane of my life.

And then there was my boss.

Shall we say we didn't get on? There were about zero things I could do right.

Despite being the most profitable member of the team consistently, I was told that I either had the wrong attitude…or an untidy desk (he wasn't wrong there) …or I didn't ask for the business enough…or I chatted too much… or I used the wrong envelope (true story) …or I made it look too easy.

HR got involved but didn't really. It was one of those things I just had to put up with. Apparently, it was even worse that every time an incentive came out, I seemed to win it quickly. Apparently, that made me lazy and only out for myself (Of course, I know now, there were most probably some other mystical and magical forces at play). Like the time when the 2 pink cars that had been in stock for nearly a year suddenly came with a bottle of pink champagne to the first salesperson that sold them (I won them both), and the trip to Barcelona, the iPod, the spa day- all me! And he didn't like it one bit.

It all took its toll, but on paper I was smashing it at life. £50k car on my driveway, money to do nice things (if only I had the time), a grown-up proper house, and now a fiancé. Despite all of this, my body was suffering. My back was so tight. My weight fluctuated. I was angry a lot of the time. I was overwhelmed, undermined and over it.

But wasn't this what I dreamed of?
Surely life isn't meant to be so relentless?
Surely there is more to it than this?

Maybe if I worked harder. Maybe if I showed up better. Maybe if I bought this thing, got that gadget, went there on holiday, or read that book then things would just get better?

My brain told me it was me. Something in me was pushing me for more. But all I knew about more was more productivity, more work, more trying. More external. More, well, masculine. The stop, the feminine, the receiver, the rest- those were weaknesses to be overcome. How was it then that the more I tried, the less satisfied I actually was? The more I pushed, the less I felt. The more I tried to fill this hole, to satisfy my targets, the emptier I felt.

How could I have known there were miracles coming just around the next corner?

And that's when my mum leant me this little book.

The Cosmic Ordering Service

Apparently, there's an invisible world out there. Apparently, we can call upon parking fairies to give us a parking space wherever we are - even in central London. Apparently, if we think about a thing, and trust it is going to come, the cosmos will deliver.

Hmmmm…
This sounds like fun. So, I went to try it out.

We were planning our wedding at the time. Having walked into a beautiful venue locally during a training course of all things, I fell in love with the place.

'I see us getting married here', I declared as I went home. We went to visit, and it was settled. Within budget? Yes! Capacity? Perfect. Accessibility? Brilliant.

From the vendors to the wedding paraphernalia, things were flowing and moving into place seamlessly. It was as if everything that I had joyfully expressed I would like was showing up. We were in the flow, expecting all the amazing things to happen- and they did…

There was just one thing.

I wasn't keen on the actual room where the ceremony was going to be held. I wanted an outdoor wedding, which was theoretically fine, but an English country wedding in May was risky.

But I knew better.

I held the vision. Every time I thought about the ceremony, I saw us outdoors, people smiling, and a warm sun in the bright blue sky. The chairs laid out on the lawn. Me walking down the beautiful steps (without falling over)- a real fairy-tale.

One week before the wedding, we have the largest rainfall May had ever seen, but I was still giddy with confidence (maybe all the wine tasting helped?!). Then the wedding planner tells me,

"It needs to be dry for two days before or the chairs will sink. If it's wet on the day, it will be in that room."
"No", I say, *"we will be outside, trust me! I've read this book you see..."*

She wasn't convinced and she wanted me to agree to plan B. That was the likely outcome after all…

Ummmm…no.

2 days before the wedding, the rain slows down. It's dry– hurrah!

The day of the wedding? The hottest day of the year. Not one cloud in the sky, the chairs laid out as I had envisaged, and the happy (and hot) people meandering on the lawn. The day went without a hitch (excuse the pun). It was the most glorious day of our life. Everything flowed, we danced, we drank, we sang, we ate. My loved ones were all there. The harpist strumming the angelic tunes. The dance-floor filled with joy. I have never smiled so much in my whole life.

I think this book thing works!

Now I was hooked. Now I was sure that I could make things happen, just through the power of my brain! The next stop in our married life was our once in a lifetime honeymoon- South Africa, Australia and Bali, here we come!

Arriving in South Africa at the Tandatula Reserve in the Timbavati was the most incredible feeling. You could hear the wild and taste it in the air. The whole space was set up for one intention: to immerse you in the natural order of things. It was as if we couldn't be further from what we were used to back home.

On our first safari trip, our driver told us how this was going to work: 2 drives a day, we go where we are led, they can't guarantee anything, and only the lucky ones get to see the big 5.

I, as I have just learned… am one of the lucky ones.

I was probably very annoying to my campmates, as this (very obvious) newlywed grinned and announced that we WILL see all the animals, you mark my words *('I had read a book, you know')*. Sure enough, on day one, our driver turned a corner and right there was the elusive leopard.

Nothing can really prepare you for witnessing these strong elegant cats in their natural environment. We all sat with bated breath, just watching this beautiful creature going about his regular business. The camera was out. And then he stood, as if posing just for us, front paws elevated on a perfectly placed log, practically screaming- '*you may take my picture*'.

We get back to camp and everyone tells us how lucky we are for seeing the leopard. Some people that were going home the following day hadn't seen one in their whole time there. '*Wow*', I thought again, '*maybe this thing does work.*'

On the next 2 trips we were greeted by the elephant, a herd of buffalo by the waterhole, two rhinos, a hippo, countless impala, zebra and giraffe, as well as the night owls and hunting birds. I wasn't expecting to feel like I did. This vulnerability and awe of being in front of the largest and potentially deadly animals in the world. It is humbling, and astounding, and silencing. The humans weren't in control. We were driving and hoping. We made way for the animals to do their thing. The elephant and her baby eating at a tree. A standoff with a huge male elephant. At the mercy of nature. We had just one drive left. And just one animal we hadn't yet seen- the lioness.

But I knew. I knew we wouldn't be leaving South Africa without being before the lions. And this, the last morning, everything was quiet. A few giraffes scattered here and there, but nothing. And then I heard the 2 way radio go off, we made a turn off the beaten track. We turned a corner and right there was not one, not two, but a whole pride of lions, lionesses, and their baby cubs, all sleeping in the sunshine. What a sight. My whole body became alive. This was… spectacular, awe inspiring, phenomenal, and unbelievable.

I am not sure what happened to me in that moment, except for something- that we appeared to have experienced the one thing that we had set our minds to. Something we couldn't control and manipulate. Something we couldn't make happen… yet it happened. Unlikely as it was, these animals, the land, the people had seemingly conspired to make this happen.

This cannot just be luck. This is so much more than luck. I wonder what other miracles will come into my life.

Ordering From The Cosmos

Naturally the 'little' discovery of ordering what we want from the Universe was opening doors to me. At that time, I still had my science and psychology brain in the driver's seat. After all, I had witnessed through the influence of my Nana, quite how magnificent the mind was. I also understood the basic NLP constructs that our Mind (Neuro), is influenced by our words (Linguistic), which creates our world view and actions (Programming). I couldn't quite understand about how the outside forces played into this. At that time, I did boil things down to coincidence and maybe a bit of cosmic magic, but it was more of a science experiment to me.

I thought; therefore, it would be a good idea to take notice of my language. I read a number of NLP books that I borrowed from my Nana's bookshelf. I noticed that there were times I was really quite mean to myself. I noticed there were times when I expected an outcome. I noticed that I saw the world and didn't really allow myself to feel it. I began to notice where I created limitations, influenced by the circumstances around me, where I gave away my power to others who could therefore control whether I had a good or bad day.

I started to reframe things. Like when I was getting comments from the boss, I changed it to a game. 1 point if it was *that* look, 2 points if it was generally aimed everyone but really aimed at me (so I thought), and 3 points if it was a direct insult or calling out. I wrote it down, I actually looked forward to them because now it was just something that happened. It was outside of me, and it wasn't influencing my inner world in quite such a dramatic way.

I noticed what I thought of myself wasn't usually the same as what the reality was, and I also noticed that at times I could brave it and change it. I would tell myself that I would talk to the right people today that will make my day enjoyable and that often resulted in a sale. I caught myself from time to time when I was being mean to myself and sometimes managed to stop.

I figured that even if this thing wasn't supernatural. That if it was just coincidence, and the power of a positive mind, then what have I got to lose. Surely being kinder to myself, having a positive outlook about what the day brought, not taking things so personally had to be better than dreading the day and assuming that life hates me. What if I cultivated the knowing that life does indeed, truly love me. And that things were consistently working in my favour? Surely, that is NLP in action. My brain giving me different thoughts, my words becoming more open and positive, can only lead to better actions I take. Surely, this things worth trying on for size.

My love for psychology and the human mind was rekindled. My science and business brain were satisfied. I was learning something more than the art of sales; I was learning the art of being human. From parking spaces to good weather days, winning tickets and incentives and general good luck, magic seemed to be around each corner.

It's Got My Back

Self-care is important; it always was for me. Back then meant a monthly massage with a local therapist. One day, I found this new girl who had put an ad in the paper. I booked her and her hands were just so magical that I felt some of the tension begin to slip away from my shoulders.

I had had a bad back my whole life as far as I remember. Diagnosed as a number of things by a number of therapists - hyper-mobility (*don't do yoga, they told me*), curve in my spine, extra ribs, how I carry my bag… no one got to the bottom of it, and it was something I just dealt with. Working my job, tottering around in high heels all day, as well as feeling as if I carried the whole world on me wasn't usually picked up by the professionals, yet I intuitively knew that it couldn't help.

One evening I am having a massage. She ends the treatment by laying her hands just above my head, the heels of her hands gently resting on my forehead. I had a feeling that my head was filling up with this beautiful kind of pressure. Like it was compacting with something that had a weight that was so comforting and gentle, that every worry and thought just seemed to stop for a moment.

It must have been a minute later that this feeling compounded, and then *whoosh*, it lifted everything out of my head. I had not felt clarity and space like this in a long, long time.

Errrrrr, what?

"What did you just do?"
"Reiki." She said.
"That felt.... I don't know, but that felt.... I got to have some more!"

And so, I booked her in. Honestly, that first session I spent half the time thinking nothing was happening and the other half wondering why I could feel heat, comfort, peace and relief. I added Reiki to my massage every few weeks and began to notice something.

On one particularly busy day, I had a customer due to pick up a car that was more than £100,000. By far the highest value car I had ever sold. It was being prepped at the very last minute (remember I said the other departments didn't care so much for the sales crew). Very apprehensively, the young technician came up to me,

"Um, Mel- that car, it's not going to be ready."
"OK," I said, a little disappointed, *"I'll deal with it."*
"Are you OK?"
"Huh? Yeah, why?"
"I thought you'd freak".
"Well, there's not much we can do, and I'll make alternative arrangements."

And that was that. Until I thought about it.

Why didn't I freak out? Why didn't I go into my usual knee jerk, stressed out, this is not good enough reaction? Why wasn't my belly turning around in knots, my head telling me that everyone and everything is incompetent and that I just always have to sort out everything myself? (huff)

Oh… I had Reiki yesterday… maybe that's it.

And that *was* it. That was when I noticed the power of this seemingly 'extra' add on that I bolted onto the end of a massage just to milk another half an hour of me time once a month. No big moment. No profound visitation from an Angel. No burning sensation. Just a gentle realisation that somehow, now, I can just handle life a little bit better.

By the way, the car? Turned out the guy couldn't make it that day and was going to call to rearrange but he forgot because he was busy, so it all worked out well in the end.

It was sometime later that the **big** thing happened with Reiki. My back at the time was really bad. The pressure at work was awful. I had a new line manager, and it wasn't working out so well. I felt that everyone was going against me. My best buddy up-line had gone to another site for a while, and I felt all alone. But I was starting to get into the self-help scene a bit more. I was rekindling my love of psychology; I was accepting that Reiki was helping me cope, and my science brain didn't know how to explain it away. I was also getting really good at the parking angel thing I had read about, and had some 'fluky' weather on days out.

This one particular winter evening, I was having a massage, and Clair, my amazing therapist, placed her hands on my shoulders when I felt it. I can only compare it to something like out of the film *The Green Mile*. It felt as if every single grain of gunk that had accumulated in my shoulders was being pulled out by her skilled hands. I was getting lighter and lighter. I am pretty sure I was trembling, and then *flash*! It felt like a bolt of lightning shot down my spine and my leg. I twitched and she removed her hands, ending the session.

What. Just. Happened?

I couldn't talk. She didn't say anything. I paid and she left, as if it was just another regular session.

Who knew that moment would be such a catalyst of change for me.

The next morning when I woke up, I had zero pain in my back for the first time in my life. Nothing. My shoulder is free, I can breathe properly! *What on Earth?* What's more, is this feeling lasted. The next day and the next. A lightness in my body, a freedom in my movement. Some sort of magic had just occurred, I was sure of it.

We went on holiday to Cuba a few days later. Now this was around 2007. Not many people spoke or knew of Reiki at that time, yet I found myself at the beach bar, sipping on the cocktail of the day in a swimsuit and hat, speaking with a stranger about my experience. A woman who, it turns out, also happens to practice Reiki. Yes, she confirms, miracles like this do happen!

I was pretty dumbfounded, as you can imagine. A whole lifetime of pain…gone. Just like that.

Until the flight home.

Approximately 10 hours on a cramped and very full flight, bitten by every mosquito within a 3 mile radius, (I had to go to the pharmacy halfway through the holiday due to the boulders that appeared on my arms from a trio of nasty bites), I started to get twitchy. I woke up the following morning to go back to work and my back was the worst it had been for a long, long time. The story I told myself was this was payback for being pain free for a week.

I know now this was my body trying to tell me something.

Up early, straight into a customer appointment at work, and I started to feel really queasy. I could hardly stand up. I was as white as a sheet, in pain from my back and now I thought that I was about to lose my guts all over the paperwork of the car I was meant to be handing over.

They didn't normally 'like' sick days so I must have really looked bad, as they actually sent me home (*maybe one day I'll tell you about the time they wouldn't let me go home when I had tonsillitis, only for my boss to call in sick 2 days later with the same symptom*s).

Anyhow, for the risk of TMI, let's just say I spent the next 7 days emptying my system. Having been signed off for a week, unable to eat, and hardly able to drink, there wasn't much I could do but just be with me and rest. But it seems I had purged more than the food. During that week, it transpired that I purged the weight I was carrying- the expectation of pleasing people and the thought that my management team actually owed me anything. I also purged the inflammation and whatever it was I was carrying in my shoulders and my neck.

From that day on, I was free from the pain that had plagued me for so long. I was no longer having to lie on tennis balls and crack my neck. But there was something else too; things flowed. I was selling cars easier than ever, I was winning prizes and sales leagues, I wasn't being harassed so much and my colleagues were joking that everything I touched turned to gold.

I wonder if this was Alchemy happening? This was the start of something greater flowing through me. I had no idea where it would lead to next.

Why Not Me?

Life continued along its flow. I was by now married and returned back from a month off work- which had given me space to start to formulate a future. A 50-hour week of working didn't really play a part in that either. Having my regular Reiki sessions was keeping me afloat. The inquiry around the NLP techniques was fascinating me. I was reading more books around mind practices and some inspirational texts. Work was ok, but now I was seeing a possibility of starting to maybe even train some people someday. It turned out that was a dream for me, and that excited me. It even made some of the hardships of the job more bearable because now it was a training ground that I could use for some future career that I had seeded in my mind. Things were moving- a little.

But then, following a massage and Reiki treatment, my godsend who was Clair, sat me down and said,

"Melissa, I've got something to tell you…"
The room started spinning.
"I am leaving the UK to go to Australia."
"Nooooooooooooooooooooooo! You can't leave me!" I cried.
"You and your magic hands are keeping me afloat. You cannot leave!"

Yet no amount of convincing from my part could sway her. (Come on Law of Attraction!) But it was what she said next that changed everything for me.

"Maybe you could learn Reiki?"

Me?

I didn't even know that was a thing. I thought you were born with it or that it was some big secret society or that... I don't know. I am not sure I even thought about how she got that gift.
"You're spiritual Mel, you can do it."

Me? Spiritual? I truly didn't see it. I was a scientist. A salesperson. A philosopher, yes. But spiritual? I had denounced religion all those years ago. Was that not the same thing? I didn't have faith, I had evidence. Spiritual was the last word I used to identify myself.

Turned out what I thought and what others thought were two different things.

Maybe I gave off a vibe.

And so, a series of wonderful and unexpected synchronicities led me to find my Reiki teacher after answering a phone call that 'wasn't my job' and taking the extra 2 minutes of my life to try and help the person at the other end of the phone. When she read out her email address- @holistictherapy- my whole-body goosebumped.

"Do you teach Reiki?" I asked her.
"Not me, but a friend who is just down the road from where you work does."
I took her number and made a call.
"Hi, I am interested in Reiki training?"
"Ah, yes. I am running one next weekend, could you make it?"

Now, I literally had one weekend off every 6 months, and they were usually filled with whatever 20-something newlyweds did on the weekend. But that weekend happened to be my one weekend off. By some miracle, I had no plans.

My body knew there was something going on here before the rest of me caught up, especially my mind. Before I knew it, I was booked on, researching what Reiki actually was, and wondering what was actually going to happen this weekend (if anything).

Who knew that this would be the start of the rest of my life,

Turns out this synchronicity thing is a real phenomenon. It is as if, when we are on our path, when we trust and follow those little nudges (or outright shoves) that come from within, the Universe seems to deliver these magical helpers- be it through the right people, or circumstances, or situations- conversations we overhear, books falling on our lap, chance encounters, all magically appearing to help us along the way.

It's pretty mind blowing really. To think how divinely orchestrated it must be. How did I know to answer that phone call? What led me to then enquire I could help her further, even though the department was shut? Where did the confidence of asking a random customer at the end of the phone if she taught Reiki come from, and how did she know that the lady who was to be my teacher happened to be teaching Reiki on my day off?

Was this magic in action?

So What Is Reiki Exactly?

Reiki is a Japanese healing technique. Although it has been around in various forms for over 1000 years, the Reiki as we know it was discovered around 100 years ago by a Sensei (Master) Usui, who was on a quest for enlightenment. After meditating upon Mount Kurama in Japan for 21 days and nights with the intention of experiencing enlightenment, he received what he was looking for on the 21st day in the form of a great white light.

The story goes that as he was rushing down the mountain to tell others of what he experienced, he stubbed his toe and as he placed his hand upon his injury, he felt this wonderfully warm healing sensation, thus discovering the healing potential this energy brought.

With this miraculous medicine he held in his hands, he had an intention for this method to reach the world and created a way of passing on the teaching to others. To cut a long, but very interesting story short, Reiki continued in its evolution and eventually reached Hawaii, where it was passed on by a formidable woman called Madame Takata. After a slow start, the powers of Reiki eventually started to gain traction and now there are tens of thousands of Reiki practitioners across the globe.

Reiki means Universal Life Force Energy, and essentially taps into this Universal energy system to bring healing and balance to those that allow for its energy to flow through them. Working on our bodies natural ability to heal, the Reiki brings our body into rest and repair, allowing for the subtle energy body, the meridians and our organs to do what they need to do to bring us back into wholeness.

Master Usui described Reiki as the 'Miraculous Medicine of All Diseases'. Personally, I found this quite a bold claim back in the day. My brain wondered how it was possible that waving your hands over someone- or bringing light touch to one's body- was able to heal… everything!! Yet, I had experiences I couldn't quite work out with my logic…

Based on 5 Principles, Reiki asks its initiates to subscribe to the following-

Just for Today, I will not anger.
Just for Today, I will not worry.
Just for Today, I will be kind to all beings.
Just for Today, I will be grateful for all things.
Just for Today, I will do my work honestly.

Now, quite frankly, when I first heard that (luckily in my training, rather than the brief research I did before) I thought that this system maybe isn't for me! I mean, I get really angry about a lot of things- the state of the world; the way the media reported certain events; the way I was being treated in various relationships and work; the way someone reacted to the thing I said, and how unfair this or that is (I don't remember exactly what, but I am sure it was important at the time!).

Don't worry? Fat chance. I am literally programmed to be worried about my sales targets; about the future; about how x might respond to y; about the traffic I might be caught up in; about whether or not this or that is killing me...

And really- grateful for *all* things.? When you say *all*... do you mean, *everything*? What about injustice, what about unfairness, what about illness, what about loss? All? Things?

Kindness? Yes, I get that. But to *all* life? What about if someone is just mean? Does that include *that* boss? I have been taught that I need to stand up for myself in life, so if I am kind to them doesn't that mean they have won? Shouldn't I be worried about that?

And honesty? It's a dog-eat-dog world out there, right? We are all out for ourselves. If we can claim something as our own, get away with selling the extra product, putting ourselves first, a little white lie or finding the easy way out- isn't that considered not just OK, but winning at life? Is that honest?

It felt like just a nice scripture. And I for one wasn't sure about how this could lead to any miraculous healing of all diseases. Sounded to me like the only way this could be achieved is to go sit up a mountain for all eternity and not have anything come to ruffle my feathers.

There are just too many circumstances that don't allow for those conditions. Maybe it's for everyone *apart* from people in the motor trade... *Anyway, back to Reiki.*

If you have never had Reiki, it's not so easy to explain, but somehow it just makes things feel better. It brings this calm sense that everything is going to be OK- even if just for a moment. I wondered if learning Reiki would help me become Zen like how I perceived the two other 'Reiki people' I knew in my life. *Here's hoping!*

Turns out too that anyone can learn Reiki. And nowadays there are plenty of forms of Reiki, including Usui, Angelic, Karuna,

Seichem, Dragon, Holy Fire and Kundalini, amongst others. All containing a slightly different frequency if you like, but with this intention of healing and bringing us back to centre.

When you learn, you are essentially dialling into this network of healing, like a radio station that is always out there in the airwaves. You dial into the frequency of Reiki (channel 111.1FM I'd like to think), and then you can bring this energy through you and into others.

Not everyone who learns Reiki does so to become a healer. Many learn just for their own curiosity, healing- and much like Master Usui himself– enlightenment; whatever that means to the individual.

Reiki One tunes you in, Reiki Two activates the symbols within you, and Reiki Three allows you to teach and pass this system on down a lineage stemming from Master Usui- in the form of an attunement. Once attuned, you then have access to this infinite source of life force energy that can be used for healing, empowerment, meditation, and a whole lot more.

Reiki has been known to bring profound feelings of peace, joy, and happiness, as well as aiding many on their spiritual path. What I didn't fully appreciate at the time is that Reiki also serves to help heal you of those things that are separating you from this natural state of wholeness and can bring refinement to our beliefs, our traits and our way of being.

Naturally, I was intrigued. Naturally, I was also pretty convinced that I would go for this training, and nothing would happen. (You see, I knew all about the placebo effect, and surely that is all that this was!?). Naturally I went, and allowed, just for today, to be open to the possibilities that awaited me.

The Initiation

Arriving at this beautiful house just a few miles from home, the smell of incense and freshly baked bread wafted through a delightfully purple, womb-like room, filled with amethyst churches and pictures of a Japanese guy on the wall. I took my pew on a comfy bean bag and settled down.

"Any questions before we start?" The teacher asked.

My head started spinning inside. *Ummmm, yes…about 1000! How does it work? Where does it come from? Will this really work for me? What if it doesn't? What is it going to change for me? Will it stop me from getting so stressed? Will it mean I will end up with a house painted purple and filled with crystals (*ask me about the crystals a few years on!*)? Is it real? Who's that guy on the wall? Is it a religion, and am I allowed to do this? Do I need to meditate? How do you pronounce Usui? What even is Usui…?*

Compose yourself Melissa.

"Errr, yes, I have **one** *(ha)- does Reiki always have to go through the hands? Last night I experienced something a bit odd. I was lying in bed, and I felt this warm breeze on the back of my head where my hairline is. I couldn't understand it. There was no source to this heat, but I could easily feel it even with my hands."*

"Reiki knows." She smiled.

(My sceptic head couldn't help but wonder what exactly Reiki knows, but I just nodded politely and carried on.)

We started speaking for a while. What to expect, why we were there, what we hoped for. I was just happy for my weekend off, but also, I wanted to be able to experience what I did after my sessions with Clair. All. The. Frickin. Time. (Is that what will happen- Zen master in a weekend?)

Then the nature of dis-ease came up. Ah yes, I nodded, that's how Nana speaks of illness- an un (dis) ease in your system. I'd seen things clear up with the power of the mind, maybe *this* is how Reiki works.

Now, it so happens that the one other person on this course, Cherry, was more cynical than I was. A scientist by profession, sent by her mum who thought it would help, she wasn't really buying any of this.

"How can our mind make our body ill? What about a broken leg?" She asked, arms crossed and a slight frown.

Have you ever said, "*I need a break*?" and then you don't listen to yourself? Something is listening. And if you don't take the break, yet you keep on telling yourself that you need one- maybe eventually your body listens and goes- *here we go then*- now you have got to actually take a load off for 6 weeks whilst you heal.

Have you ever described someone as a pain in the neck? Then found when they come to stay the weekend you can't turn your head. Have you ever found something '*hard to swallow*', or been '*sick of something*', or even said that '*something is killing you*?'

All my bells and whistles are firing off at this. This is NLP 101. This intrinsic connection between what we say to ourselves and our body taking everything literally. How many times had I swallowed my words and wondered why I suffered with frequent throat infections? How many times had I not listened to advice or guidance, or even my own self, and regularly found myself with blocked ears? How many times did I need to get something off my chest and then be struck down with a cough? And wow, did I feel I had the weight of the world on my shoulders, so no wonder that part of me was so tight.

Ok- you have my attention. I understood and sought to explain this to my colleague here who was not having any of it.

I still wasn't sure at this point what any of that had to do with Reiki, or if we were actually talking about another phenomenon, but was loving the conversation regardless. Reiki, she tells me, works with the energy of all of this to help heal. If the dis-ease can start as a thought, then when we bring healing, it can help to change that thought, and so change the physical manifestation of it.

Ooooookay. (Or it's the placebo!- did you know I am a smarty pants and I like to know- and be able to explain– everything?)

"Now it's time for your attunement. I am going to take you upstairs one by one; you'll feel me touching you, and some blowing, and I'll move your hands, and then you will be attuned into Reiki."

Now, this is where it all got a bit weird for me. I couldn't quite understand how I could go from lay person with zero magic powers- you tickle my head and blow into my hands and then I am 'attuned'. Let's see.

"Set your intention," she says. I think my words were something like, *"I hope this works and I am open to the possibility that this*

will do something." I closed my eyes, and when I opened them again only a few minutes later, things were different.

The first words out of my mouth were, *"Weird..."*
"What happened?" she asked.
"I dunno. The room looks like it's got little dots all in it." I felt a warmth or a pressure around me. I saw some funky colours- mainly green, and I feel... different.

My hands for the first time in as long as I remembered were actually warm. Everyone who shook my hand up to that point would comment that I had cold hands. *'Cold hands, warm heart'* they would say because mine were always cold, no matter what. I kind of floated down the stairs. Whilst Cherry was receiving her attunement, I played with this new energy connection. I played with how it felt in the area between my hand and my leg. Curious, it was warm and fuzzy. I placed two fingers in the middle of my palm which were suddenly itchy and felt like a breeze emitting from it.

I looked around the room. Were things brighter? Had the sun come out? Was that crystal quite so sparkly and attractive before?

Something was different, and *this* time I didn't have the answers.

I was instructed to scan my hands around the body of the other trainee that day and just notice what I experienced. I started to get a tingle in my hands around certain areas, like my hand had been stuck in an analogue TV and was fizzing all around. It was pretty astounding how all of a sudden now I was aware of something that looked invisible, but I could actually feel it in my hands.

When I reached the top of her arm, I found myself just coming to a stop. A little like my hand had subtly magnetised to that spot. The static feeling started, and my teacher instructed me to leave my hand there, to tune in, and notice what happened. The feeling began to intensify and then I had an image of a double bass or some sort of large musical instrument. All the while I was reiterating to the room exactly what I was experiencing.

"Does that mean anything to you?" My teacher asked Cherry,
"No", Cherry replied.
"Any tension in your arm?"
"No."

I was a little disheartened that I had not picked up something majorly profound, yet I *knew* that I had felt *something*. I was keen to learn more. And if that wasn't strange enough. We then got the blindfolds out (Err).

"Place your hands around these three objects. Tell me what you feel and sense."

I wasn't sure exactly, but they definitely felt different from each other. Different sensations going on in my hands, different images and colours in my mind's eye. I kind of guessed that one was a crystal (*did I guess?*) but was surprised to see the can of baked beans and the other an unlit candle. NB: My teacher later admitted to me that this was the very first time in the history of Reiki training that she had ever even considered getting out a can of baked beans. Glad she did though, because it worked for me!

Those two days were so nurturing. The energy soft and slow. The food homemade and nourishing. The conversation deep and profound. The practices experiential and revealing. During one discussion, Cherry said,

"I injured my arm years ago when I was playing in the orchestra and sometimes it plays up."
"What did you play?" I gasped, excitement rising from my belly.
"The cello!" She replied, the grin of realisation slowly moving up her face.

Erm, did I just have my first psychic experience? Did Reiki somehow just convey to me that there was indeed an old injury or imbalance in her arm, and it was linked to playing a large string instrument? (I mean, who actually knows the difference between a cello and a double bass anyway?)

Mind blown. No explanation. This is definite sorcery. What is going on?!

I think my teacher was so pleased that at least one of us was getting it, and she was so encouraging. We were practicing on each other and on her. I was now like a sponge, wanting to know (and explain) all these things to which there was no explanation for. I was becoming convinced that there was something so profound going on. There was no way life could ever be the same again.

And so, I was doing what I do best- asking the big questions. Where does it come from? Does it run out? What does this mean? How does it work? Is reality even as I know it? Does this mean the *Celestine Prophecy* that I read as a teen was *actually* a true story? What else am I missing? What was that green energy that was with me? Angels? What?

And then we start to talk about the nature of reality! Yes, I say, I have a parking Angel (proudly). What else do I need to know?

And so, I was sent away with a reading list- *The Power of Now* by Eckhart Tolle, *The Alchemist* by Paulo Coelho, Abraham

Hicks and- the one that made me get that feeling- *Seth Speaks* by Jane Roberts.

Homeward I go. It's time for my weekly Nana call and I tell her all about the profound experience I had just encountered.

The next three weeks I was a bit obsessed. Hands on, Reiki on! ... so, my hands were on; *all the time*. I fell asleep with Reiki, I watched TV with Reiki, I held Mark's hand with Reiki, I cooked with Reiki, I sat with Reiki, I worked with Reiki. Filling me up to the very brim with Reiki. It was absolutely divine. This feeling of fullness in my stomach. I felt untouchable. This power coursing through my hands, I wanted to tell the world about it but wasn't quite sure how, without sounding like a nut.

Until one Saturday morning 3 weeks later, when I walked into that beautiful showroom and my whole body hurt. It was as if the walls of the place were screaming out to me *"Get out of here! LEAVE!"* It was like being pounded by an invisible force of nature. I could feel it and I could hear it, and I just knew that this time I meant it.

In the 7 or so years I worked in that showroom, I must have said on at least 63,872 occasions that I was going to leave. I had even had interviews for various other prestige jobs but knew even then that it would be a case of different circus, same performance, so I never took the leap. Besides, there were things I absolutely loved about where I worked. My colleagues were my besties, the cars were the best in the world, and I would get a new one (cleaned every Friday) for free(ish) every three months. The pay was great, the benefits were great, the training was world class and there's a buzz about working in the motor industry that I am not sure you get anywhere else. Besides, I was making people's dreams come true wasn't I, and that was what I always wanted.

But that day it was different. So, I bowled up to reception- the same place I was when I took that phone call not more than 6 weeks before, that led me to my Reiki teacher, sat down and said to the receptionist for the umpteenth time,

"*I gotta leave.*"

Lying there was the local paper that had just been delivered. I opened it up to the middle, and the first page I saw was a full-page ad for a company that was local, that was into training and support, and was in the industry that I had known for so long. The job description was vague, but I pointed and went, "*There. That's where I am going.*"

6 weeks later I was offered the job.

And now it was decision time.

Do I leave this job I love and hate? A job that I am damn good at, that right now means I am driving my absolute dream car, a friggin' soft top convertible and that pays me well, to go to this other job that I know very little about, with no car, a huge 50% pay drop and a drop in perceived status.

What on Earth do I do? Of course, then the sales start rolling in. Something is trying to convince me that it's not so bad here after all; but that feeling every time I walked in wouldn't go away.

The new firm, however needed an answer, and it was crunch time. My husband was just super supportive (so no help at all!) and told me to do what I needed to. He confirmed that we would be ok with the money drop; it was more important that I was happy.

The 50-hour weeks were taking its toll, and this was a regular 9-5 with an actual lunch break! Luxury! It also meant that I could pursue this passion that was building; to train or coach others. I had even taken a free 2-day coaching course, taking my last precious days holiday the week before, which I loved to bits, and everyone I practiced with was telling me I was a natural.

"SOMEONE TELL ME WHAT TO DO!" I screamed into the night.

Lying in bed, preparing myself for what was inevitably going to be a sleepless night as I make a decision. I did what I was now used to doing; placing my Reiki hands on my belly I let the energy flow through me, and I did what anyone who was brought up within religion (and since rejected it) did: I prayed.

"Dear God, please help me. I don't know what to do. Help me make a decision. What is best? Do I stay? Do I go? I don't want to be wrong here."

The radio was playing, though I wasn't even listening to it. Lost in my thoughts, swimming around my mind, and then I heard it:

'*You got a fast car.*
Is it fast enough so we can fly away?
We gotta make a decision,
Leave tonight and live and die this way.'
(Tracy L. Chapman - Fast Car)

And in that moment, I knew. The next morning, I did the scariest thing I had done to date: I handed in my notice.

The Motivation

What surprised me the most when I was called up to the Ivory Tower to discuss my resignation, was how much this boss, who I had convinced myself hated the living bones out of me for the last few years, was trying to persuade me to stay.

He quizzed me about the new role, asking why I would give up such a wonderful opportunity that I had right here, and was bewildered about why I was choosing to move down at least 3 pay grades.

"I want to do something that makes a difference", I told him. *"I want to go and study NLP and Coaching skills. I want to go and train other people; that is what inspires me. I can't do that working all these hours."*
"
What if we gave you more weekends off?" He enquired.

Now I am sitting there close to tears. It was like everything I had wished for over the last probably 2 years was now on the table. Maybe my belief that this man disrespected me and would have preferred to never lay eyes on me again might have actually of been wrong. Was it in my mind? Or were all the little talks, looks and comments, his idea of motivation?

I think a part of me was touched. I wavered for a moment.

"What is it you want Melissa?" Staring directly at me.

"I want to help people. I want to help people be the best they can be. I want to work when I want, with who I want and how I want. I want to work for me. I want freedom."

And do you know what he did? He laughed in my face. He took my dreams, screwed them up in a ball, spat on them and laughed.

"You live in a dream world, Melissa. If you work for yourself, you'll be travelling up and down the country chasing work, taking on things for the money. You think it's easy doing that? It's delusional."

I heard him. I heard his belief; I heard the desperation. And I also heard a quiet voice inside that said:

"That's not your truth Melissa. That's not your truth."

So, tears in my eyes, a pain in my heart and butterflies in my belly, I walked out of there knowing that something had changed in me.

The Stories We Tell Ourselves

Have you ever noticed that life seems to serve you up what it is you thought you wanted, right when we have made the decision to take another road?

What is that all about?

It's as if the Universe wants to really makes sure that this is what you actually want. That you're not just doing it off the cuff. That you are so sure (when is anyone so sure really?) that there will be no stopping you. In fact, it happens so often even my new boss, whilst I was having the second interview, asked me what I would do if the old company offered me a new contract. In fact he did, and it made me question it: What is it I actually want?

It is so normal to waiver in these moments; of course, it is. The thing is, we have spent so long telling ourselves stories of what we think is actually happening, It isn't until someone, or something challenges the status quo, that we get snapped out of the spell we were under,

I spent so long telling myself a story of who I was in the role I was in. Creating a reality that said I was bullied, or at least harassed. That I was hard done by. That my colleagues thought of me in a certain way, that my boss hated me. That the 'boys' thought I was useless, and *'it doesn't matter how hard I try, or how well I do, they'll never be happy'*.

How could I be surprised when that was what life served me?

I wonder how I would have behaved if I knew that my boss did indeed hold me in high regards. What would have happened then? Maybe I would have been more satisfied? Perhaps. Maybe I would have sold more, or less. Maybe I never would have gone searching for something else. Maybe, I would never have had the conversation in the previous chapter, which stayed with me long after the doors of that ivory tower slammed shut.

It got me wondering- how many versions of me exist? The me that is held in the eyes of my mum is very different to the me that is held in the eyes of my colleagues. My friends knew different versions of me; indeed, each of them had their own version. My husband. My children. The teachers from school. Quite how many versions are there of little me, creating thought forms in people's minds?

The mother, the daughter, the colleague, the employee, the boss, the sister, the friend, the sales person, the boss, the motivator, the listener, the advisor, the client, the shopper, the fool, the serious one, the weird one, the girl that passed you on the street. The list continues on and on.

No wonder we are all confused all the time! If we live our lives so worried about what everyone else thinks, trying to live up to everyone else's expectations; who, and what are we actually aligning to? And wow, what a waste of time trying to appease everybody, because surely, as one is impressed, or satisfied, it would only disappoint another. Then it begs the question, how could we ever change? How can we grow, and become, and evolve, if we are always trying to fit into the very boxes that someone else, everyone else, has built uncomfortably around us?

Think about how you hold others in your mind. How often you think about them. The opinions you have of them- good or bad. How they have behaved a certain way, and then, suddenly, maybe you meet them out of context, or under enormous pressure, and they behave in a completely new way. Seeing a whole new side of them. What happens then? Are you disappointed? Impressed? Confused? Where did your impression of them come from anyway? Should they be spending their lives trying to appease *you* because you hold an image of them that they may or may not have passed on to you consciously.

Does it even really matter?

I know I had spent so much time and energy so worried about what everyone else thought, I rarely brought to mind what indeed it was that *I* thought. What was right for *me*. How ideas fit in with *my* values. Where those values even came from.

The byproduct of that was this; I spent a lot of time projecting. My ideas of others, letting them trigger me. Holding expectations of how they should behave and what they should be doing. And creating all the stories in the world, that had zero basis in fact, about what it was they were saying about me.

That takes a lot of energy. Wasted energy. Constantly trying to make myself fit into a mould that only I truly created. In my head. Too scared to break free, but too uncomfortable to stay put. Which was worse? What story was I ready to begin telling?

Could it finally be my own?

If the Universe is consistently serving us on all of the projections and stories we hold. Maybe it was about time to look truthfully at them all.

The Sister Wound

Women cannot be trusted.

At least, that was a story I was very used to telling myself. At school- apart from a couple of close female friends- my mates were mainly boys. You could say I was in the 'popular' crowd, but I never felt like I fit in there. It was full of bitchiness, cattiness and gossip; a really easy and enticing trap to fall into. You see, you either agreed or were the weirdo. The quickest way to bond with many of the girls in my school- especially the ones that were *worth* knowing- was to pack together and talk about the *others*. I found myself on both sides of that fence during my 5 years of high school, and quickly learned that I couldn't really trust the cool kids. Whilst being part of the pack was seemingly safer- I could only really trust myself, even though I actually didn't know who I was...

It left me with a lifelong wounding that led me to believe that whenever I was in a group (especially of women), that they hated me, disliked me or thought I was an oddity. I capitalised on that in my mid-teens as I dressed in my Doc Martens, combat trousers and leather jacket and listened to the bands that no one had heard of; in truth, it was a front. If I can make myself weird, then it's not me they're hating- it's the idea of me. Still- in the crowd or out, I was convinced that people were looking at me in a certain way or were bitching about me behind my back. After all, life had proved that to me over and over again.

Working in the motor trade my whole adult life had given me two sides of another coin. Often the only girl in the group, I faced the jeers and the jives- which I responded to with quick witted humour (it was a gift).This was how I established myself, and it kinda worked. Somehow, I felt safer surrounded by all the guys who were what they were. I knew where I was with them. I could create good stories around them.

When I started my next job, I had to face it all again. In a building full of women, I walked into a new team. They seemed nice, but my old voice talk came back telling me they didn't like me really. I was too much. Too loud. Too quiet. Too annoying. Too experienced. Too strange. Too different.

It's interesting noticing how you behave when you think no one likes you. Me? I responded with turning on my confidence mask and hoping no one saw through it. I allowed my humour to stop anyone really getting too close.

Now, when you act like you're super confident and know what you're doing, but inside you feel like a fraudulent failure- interesting things start to happen. People respond to you in a way that doesn't feel congruent with how you think you are. It contains a lot of pressure. You make up stories in your head that are annoying at best and dangerous at worse.

It felt, to me, like an act I had to keep up, because now it had gone too far. And that is tiring.

Was there something else, deeper, going on here?

It turns out that we as women have been pitted against each other for centuries. In modern day, we see it through our movies. We feel it through the mean girls; the cackle of women coming together; the expectations we have of each other- most of which unachievable and contrary. Only a century ago, women were forced to turn against each other, to turn each other in, to mistrust. In many places, it was a crime for women to gather in more than pairs. In others we were asked to be the eyes for the authorities to report *suspicious* behaviour. When 'suspicious behaviour' could be determined as a bunch of women coming together laughing- or even worse, having an intelligent conversion- it is no wonder so many of us are left cautious, distrusting, and acting the way we often do.

We all find coping mechanisms. The old, *if you can't beat them join them* adage worked for me for some time. Whilst the bitching and the gossip might have left me with a *moment* of superiority, in truth, it just left me bitter ,and paranoid.

How could I trust anyone when I couldn't even trust myself?

I wonder sometimes which side of the fence I would have been on during the *Burning Times*. The truth is, I think it was both. It is hard to stand up to the crowd- no less if your life was on the line. For centuries we were taught that it was safer and the *'right thing'* to do to report anyone who has an opinion that differs from the Church.

So here we are, in the safest time for centuries, still acting as if being in our power isn't safe. Yet now something is different. Back then, we were severed from our communities. Our villages that were made up of women, midwives, healers, crones, and the wise ones, coming together and raising the tribe. Working with our local medicines, our local plants, sharing our wisdom and the responsibility of childhood and parenthood- of life and death. It is amazing what one generation of distrust can make us forget, let alone countless.

The damage was done, and many of us haven't ever experienced this kind of community in our lives. We live in separation. We don't trust. We give our power to the authority who, we believe, know what's best for us. Our gut is telling us it's not safe to trust. Our brain telling us we must. Our primal instincts are screaming it is not safe! So, we are confused, and we do what it is we know best to do.

We survive. And that survival sometimes comes with a bitterness that is hard to swallow. The memories of the tribal world before are starting to leave our cellular memories; our mothers, their mothers, and their mothers not having that experience. Reading how to raise children from a book written by men. Taught to hush down our mother's intuition and our need for sisterhood- because it's not right- we can't trust it, it doesn't exist... and then we are left to deal with that in an ever separated and fast-paced world.

Turns out, there were other people like me; that deep, deep, down saw through that. There were other people like me who were also so tired of wearing the mask. There were other people like me that were living so far in their masculine that a part of them was being called back. There were other people like me... it's just none of us knew about each other- we didn't even know it in ourselves.

And so, the cycles continued; until some years later, I met someone who told me about this group she went to called the Red Tent. It focused on women coming together during the new moon to share how we feel and do some activities, maybe read a poem, make things, sing, connect... I wasn't so sure.

My initial thought was that I couldn't think of anything worse. It sounded a bit, well, fake, and uncomfortable... Yet something convinced me, and she asked if I would keep her company, so I agreed to go.

I remember sitting in the circle. Some candles were lit to honour our ancestors, ourselves and our children. At the time, I had just had my 3rd child. He was only a couple of weeks old during my first meeting, so I held on to him like a safety blanket and thought,

"Well, if it all gets too much, I can always blame him and leave."

But something happened.

When the talking stone came round to me, and I was asked what I wanted to share and how I felt- something rose within me. No one had asked me how I felt- really and truly- in a long time. I hadn't considered how I felt; I was just getting on with it. I didn't even know what to say, so I tentatively dipped in, and I asked myself, for the first time in forever;

"How are you today, Melissa?"

I found out there was a lot going on under the surface of my new mum hormones that needed this outlet. That needed this connection. That needed this unfiltered, uninterrupted talking to rise from me. Words were leaving my mouth like I was in confession. I offloaded and all the other women sat around me and held me in my vulnerability.

Something happened when I heard them, all the other women sharing their hearts and souls, I found something in me too. Compassion. Non-judgement. For once, I didn't have to give them an answer, solve their problems, agree with them, find my 'me too' story, or break the silence with a joke or smart comment…

Something was happening.
Something was healing.

Over the months that followed, it became what I needed. The place to go that somehow made the rest of the month seem easier. I finally understood what it meant to have a sisterhood. A group of women that held, shared, laughed and cried. Rejoiced and mourned. Together. No judgement. No bitchiness. No competition. I had found my tribe. I had found a resource that awakened something in me. And I began to heal decades- if not lifetimes- of sister wounds that I didn't even know I carried.

I think every county should have a Red Tent community, or something similar. For me, it helped me honour and relish my womanhood. It helped me normalise my periods, my body, my hormones and my feelings. It helped me to trust again.

If every county had a Red Tent, I truly believe many of our issues will be solved. Sisterhood is something to be cherished. It is something that we need through our childhood, our menarche, our motherhood, our menopause and all spaces in between or skipped.

Here is where I learned of the maiden, the mother and the crone, and saw the magic in them all. The three phases of womanhood.

The Maiden: innocent, full of inquisitiveness, freedom, intelligence. Bursting into a life of exploration and expansion.

The Mother: the giver of life, the nurturer, the manifestor. The creatrix of life itself as she blossoms into adulthood.

The Crone: the wise woman who has lived and learned and grown. A vision of safety as she assists us whilst we transition and learn and wonder through life, guiding and watching over us, soothing and encouraging in perfect measure.

Here is where I stopped fearing the judgement of others. Here is where I found a part of me that I never knew existed. Here is where my divine feminine started to stir, awaken and feel free enough to show her face. Here is where my masculine could finally take a break. Here is where great healing happened. So, dear reader, I recommend finding a sister circle, a Red Tent, or making one of your own and honouring the concepts of this space. We share with no judgement. We listen with no advice. We hold each other with no expectation. We allow *all* of us to be.

And what happens in the Red Tent, stays in the Red Tent.

Sacred. Supportive. Sisterhood.

It's a game changer for sure.

The Inner World

There I was, navigating my way through my new position in the new company. Having known what I had given up taking this new role, I was determined that the extra 15 hours a week plus all the weekends I had gained wouldn't be put to waste. I was reading books to help me understand this Reiki thing I was starting to get *good* at. I took part in an online hypnotherapy training that my Nana had recommended to me, and I was looking into courses, often finding this or that to do on my weekends off.

It felt fated when I put in a proposal in for training in NLP. The company had a training budget and, luckily for me, there weren't many of us putting ourselves forward (*always the training enthusiast was I!*). A full NLP training course- with lifetime access was now mine- AND I got the week off work to attend!

I was also progressing through the company, being given more responsibility, travelling the country, meeting other trainers and senior managers of large businesses. I was becoming more confident within myself and my abilities. I was also NLP-ing myself when I found I was sinking back into old patterns.

Now I had a mission outside of my work too. I was learning and growing. I wanted to know it all and wasn't afraid to speak about it.

At the time I had picked up one of the recommended books my Reiki teacher had given me, called *Seth Speaks*. It is a channelled text. I had never heard of such a thing, but I was fascinated!

The book explained that the channel- Jane Roberts- started to receive this information. She would go into a trance-like (altered) state and start speaking in a voice different to her own. Her husband then took down the notes as she dictated and translated what was coming to her.

This was some deep stuff, and I was hooked. Seth would speak about how we fully create our own reality here. That something is not in fruition until we notice it and label it. And that collective experiences only happen because somehow, we agree on an outcome. (*Where have I heard this before!*)

He spoke about past lives and how they influence us. How our thoughts are not just manifesting parking fairies but creating our whole human experience. How our dream state and waking state are so intricately intertwined, and how time isn't quite what we thought it is…

Now, you can imagine that my little mind was firstly cynical and secondly curious. How my science brain is saying, *"Are you sure- a channelled text?"* But there was another part of me that was now opening up to something else. Feeling the Reiki course through my system- a reminder that this was something I couldn't believe or get my head round until I experienced it for myself.

What other wonders have I written off just because they don't fit into the mainstream?

What I did know was that I carried that book around with me everywhere. And it held an energy, even when it was closed. I could feel something when I was reading it and even though it didn't make sense, it completely made sense at the same time.

It was as if my inner world; a place that had always been so rich and deep, was being validated. All the comments at school by my teachers of needing to 'focus more because I daydreamed' and sat in the back of the class 'twiddling my hair' was more than me being 'naughty'. I was creating whole worlds- just in another reality! Who knew!

So, I set out to test out this little (big) theory.

The Secret

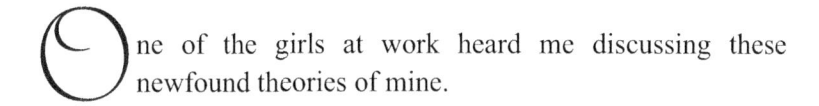

One of the girls at work heard me discussing these newfound theories of mine.

"Have you read The Secret?" she asked. I hadn't and I quickly rectified that. There in my hands was a small book with a mystical cover, complete with wax stamp, helping me to explain the inner workings of the Universe. In language much simpler than I had been focused on, it explained that I need only think of something and in that moment the thing I thought of was attracted to me. My job was to sit back and receive it.

I quickly downloaded my blank check and wrote it out to me from the Universe.

Pay Melissa Amos £1000,000
*Signed by the Universe (*thank you very much).

I'd tell my husband if he was having a quiet time at work selling cars;

"Repeat after me: *"I AM a money magnet! I AM a money magnet! I AM A MONEY MAGNET! Say it like you mean it!"* He'd come home from work the next day and invariably say,
"Yes! I sold a car!"
"You see, this shiz works!" And the Universe was proving it to me over and over again.

It was on a trip to America that things really started to get real. I was away with family- who were doctors, surgeons, lawyers and business owners- and here I am talking to them about how we can manifest anything. If we believe and we trust.

"Like how?" they asked me.
"Like, for example… (quick Melissa think) *…like, we could manifest free Disney tickets!"* I say with as much confidence as a fish…but I had said it.
"How are we going to get free Disney tickets?" she rebutted.
"By asking the Universe", I say, *"being in gratitude like you know it is coming and allow the Universe to bring it to us. BUT we cannot ask HOW, we must just know it is coming and believe it will be."*

It is entirely possible that in that moment, she and the rest of the room were wondering what sort of medical intervention was best for me. But the wine was flowing that night and somehow, we moved on from those looks.

In my head, I was wondering how this was actually going to come into fruition. But the course was set, and the intention released- and now I just had to allow.

A little less than 2 hours later, my brother took a call. He looks happy, I think. He comes into the room and exclaims:

"Guess what? We have just bagged 4 free Park Hopper Disney Tickets!"

The look on all our faces must have been priceless. He wasn't a part of the manifesting conversation. I had no idea this was on the cards. He had no idea this was going to happen. We were all sitting there a little dumbfounded.

The lawyer looks at me. WTF? Inside my tummy is flipping, dancing, expanding and I'm probably also feeling a little bit sick. And I just smile my wry smile.

"You see! This is how it works!"
What the actual...?
Wow, wow, wow, wow, wow, wow, wow!

This thing *does* actually work! I mean, that was specific, and look how quickly that happened! Free Disney tickets worth hundreds of dollars. THANK YOU, UNIVERSE! This is awesome!

On the day we went to go, I knew the Universe was on my side. It was spring break, the busiest time of the year in the parks in Florida. Yet now I wanted to prove to everyone quite how remarkable this newfound theory was.

"We will get on every ride that we want... without queuing!". (I got the look again).

So, we turn up to the Animal Kingdom and it turns out they now have these machines you can book your tickets to get on the ride. And somehow, we managed to get on (you know where this is going, don't you?) every single ride that we wanted to, straight away.

Then to the show- a mini version of the *Lion King* was on (who doesn't love the *Lion King*?). Amazingly, we managed to get into the next showing by just turning up at the right time. Feeling cocky now, I said, *"Front row anyone?"*

The theatre was pretty much full by this point. I mean we had turned up at just exactly the right time to get into the show, but I was flying high and had learned, just for today, to not put any parameters on the miracles that could happen. Just then, one of the Disney cast members says,

"Is there a party of four?"
My hand shoots up.
"Here we go, ma'am."

Guess where we were... front row, of course!

By this point I am pretty sure my family had cast me as a witch, or that I had somehow conspired to set up this course of events by some bribery and back handers, but no. I was in the flow. I was asking without wanting to figure out how, for things that would make this the best day ever! And it was. It was awesome.

Until we went to Hollywood Studios.

Now, I am not sure I have ever shared my story of how I was scared of rollercoasters. It wasn't something that had affected my life that much growing up, but on my first holiday with Mark, where we were going round the theme parks, after his brother David married his new bride Julie, when it all came to head. I didn't want to lose face, and when my future mother-in-law pointed to this huge tower and said, "Let's go on that", I couldn't really be the chicken. I was trying to prove myself to my new future family, so reluctantly I found myself strapped into this bench.

We went up. Up. Up. Up and up some more. There we were, suspended high in the air, and I knew what was coming. Something in my head was trying to convince me that a better option than sitting on this horrible thing that I knew any moment was about to free drop me down, was to unstrap myself and throw myself off. You heard that right. My brain was trying to convince me that throwing myself a 10000ft drop (it seemed) was a better option than being strapped onto this bench and endure the next 30 seconds of this torture.

I had never experienced such a feeling of dread. I was just as scared as what my mind was telling me to do to make this situation stop, as I was about the feeling that was about to manifest from being dropped from this height. But everyone else was having such a great time that I dare not make a scene, so I shut my eyes super, super tight- luckily discovering I couldn't unstrap myself anyway. Then before I knew it, it was over.

I was shaken, but then it was the bride and groom's turn to choose a ride. They pointed to the big green one over there... The Hulk. Queue time 60 minutes (I didn't know about the law of attraction, Disney fast pass hack then). My plan was this; Queue up with them and then, at the last minute before we go on, duck out and meet them on the other side.

It was a good plan.

Until I found myself being shuffled on and sitting in the middle of the row so I couldn't escape. The bars came down. We were locked in.

"Get me off! Get me off!" I screamed.

But no one heard, and if they did they weren't listening, and now it was too late. The thumb went up. The countdown began. 10. 9... (*I need to get off, I need to get off, get me the f**k off of here!*) And then the countdown suddenly went from 6 to 0 in 2 seconds flat and we were shot off at a million miles an hour. I was screaming my little head off.

The whole trip around this metal jungle- twisting and turning, dropping upside down- could only have lasted around 60 seconds, but halfway through I realised something. I couldn't go anywhere; I was there for the long haul. And actually, this was quite, well, exhilarating. So, my screams turned into whoops. I even managed to relax my tight white knuckles that were gripping on for dear life, and I began to enjoy it!

The picture that got snapped on its biggest drop after flying upside down, said it all... I was grinning from ear to ear. I felt the fear and I was doing it anyway. WOW! This was actually FUN, I get it.

"Which one next?" I said.

That was the start of my love affair with the biggest, fastest and most imaginative roller coasters in the world.

BUT....

The memory of the *Doctor Doom's Free-fall* ride from a few years before was still in there, still in my cells as I entered the Hollywood Studios. The memory of me wanting to actually launch myself off from a height was just right there at the tip of my awareness. When I saw the *Tower of Terror* looming, it all came flooding back. Turns out a coaster is fine... but an elevator style vertical free-fall was most definitely not.

"Come on", they said, *"let's go on that."*

Remember, we were used to getting straight on every ride. So, I stated, *"Only if the queue is short."* Meanwhile I was begging in my mind, *"Please let it be long! Please let it be long!"* We get to the information board and see a wait time of 75 minutes. Thankfully, we decided to leave that one (*hurrah!*), and from there the spell had somewhat broken.

Turns out the Law of Attraction works both ways.

But, wow, was I relieved! And no. before you ask, that is one fear I don't feel ready to conquer, not for this lifetime anyway.

I wonder what it was that told my body that dropping from such a great height was unsafe (I mean it is, but) ... that one is for another time.

So, it turned out the Universe was pulling out all the stops to show me how the Law of Attraction worked. To prove to me that I can magnetise to me what it is that I want. For the first time in my life, I actually felt powerful. I got an inkling that maybe this was limitless. I was on a roll! Life Loves Me! Maybe that $1000,000 was on its way after all.

But there's a price that comes with that power, and it turns out my brain isn't trained to constantly think about free tickets and everything moving in flow, and life always working in my favour.

Sometimes other things enter my head, things I didn't plan, or create, or would want in a thousand lifetimes. But they're there. Sometimes subtle, often loud, and filled with something far from the flow I had experienced on that day. Fear. Judgement. Tragedy. Shame. Things that were very hard to high vibe my way out of…

All Shook Up

On the subway, travelling under the water of San Francisco Bay and minding my own business, a thought comes into my mind.

What if there was an earthquake right now?

I had heard that the area was prone to a quake or two, and here I was on a busy BART (subway) train on the way to this beautiful built-up city, 135 feet under the bay, on this old underground system.

The innocent thought quickly turns into panic.

My thoughts create my things, and my feelings amplify it. Right now, I am doing belly flips inside, thinking my power mind is going to create an earthquake. I'm telling myself that it will be all my fault, and we are never going to get out of here alive!

I could see in my head, the water cracking through the tunnel. I could feel my feet moving. I could hear the screams.

Panic was rising.

'Melissa… snap out of this or you're going to singlehandedly cause a natural disaster right here on the subway!'

Luckily, this was where my NLP brain kicked in. The brain that registers only the positive. The brain that doesn't understand can't, don't or won't.

Lucky for me also, I am aware that this Universe works on a time lag. Don't believe me? Think of a pink elephant and be glad one doesn't apparate straight onto your sofa!

So, I breathed. I took a look at my feet, securely resting on the dirty floor, where thousands of commuters had trampled safely to reach their destinations in the past. This settled me down. So, what is the opposite of an earthquake, I asked myself?

Safety. Stillness. Calm. Having fun where I am going. So, I started there. I started by grounding into the safety I was in, in that very moment. I told myself that I am safe. I told myself that I am calm. I started to believe what I was telling myself. I then projected where I was going. I pictured emerging from the BART station, safe and sound, and seeing the bright blue skies like a canopy, high above the high-rise buildings. I pictured laughter. I imagined walking over the Golden Gate Bridge. I saw us getting a table at the Cheesecake Factory (*when in Rome*). I imagined us all going back to my aunt's house for dinner and telling them what an amazing day we had.

And that was what happened. No earthquake, just a great day. But even though I hadn't created an earthquake under the bay, I had shaken myself to the core. If I can create Disney tickets, then maybe every time my brain started doing that thing it does and offering me the worst-case scenarios, maybe I was creating that. If I let it consume me- like we so often do- then I would be creating the life I feared the most.

How do we handle that?

Trying to control these incessant thoughts and join the love and light only brigade is not only hard work, but nigh on impossible. So how do we navigate that?

Where Did That Thought Come From?

Have *you ever wondered where a thought comes from?* They say we have between 7 and 40 thoughts per MINUTE! Per minute!

Try it now. Just sit for a moment and notice what happens. Look away from the book or close your eyes and notice what it is that comes up for you. *I'll wait right here…*

Did your brain have something it wanted to tell you? What happened when you gave it space to listen? Was it a thought that you created, or did it come from somewhere else?

Because you see, I noticed in my inner earthquake moment, that the teachings of 'your thoughts create your things' might well be true, but if we aren't working on what creates our thoughts, well we might be fighting a losing battle. As I listen to mine, I noticed something. I noticed that my thoughts seemed to arise from certain places.

My past, for one. Those things that happened 5 minutes ago, 3 days ago, last year, last decade, as a child. It's as if some of these thoughts have swum around forever- never really attended to, just this background noise- reaffirming something that I apparently decided to take on as my own inner guidance system for some reason as I have travelled on my path.

Music is another one. I am not sure about you, but I often hear songs in my head. And it's not always the inspiring ones either. Quite often it's the annoying ditty that has come from some clever piece of marketing that is now swimming around my brain and subtly reinforcing the message that I should be purchasing that thing. Or I find myself singing the latest hit about how I would probably die if this person doesn't love me back, or how hard love is, or how difficult life can be (hardly healthy is it?).

Or my thoughts spring up from the news that just came on, asking me to feel bad, scared, angry, guilty, or tense. Telling me to expect the worse or how others are suffering. My brain loved to lap those ones up- compounded by everyone who came into contact with me who heard the same news and started the conversation with something along the lines of *'Isn't it awful?'* or *'What is the world coming to?'* Oh, the drama, and that inner chatter loved to remind me time and again.

Let's not forget our friends. They say that you become the sum of the people you hang around with the most. So, it's no wonder that your friend's opinions, projections, worries and intentions all swim around your mind. You love your friends and quite often you value them, so your mind gets pulled to what they've told you or, even better, what they are 'probably' thinking, saying or judging about you.

Caregivers can take up our thoughts as well. How often do we hear the voice of our parents coming out our own mouths? The beliefs around money (*it doesn't grow on trees, you know*), work, ethic, morals or behaviours. How aware were they about this Law of Attraction thing when you were in your formative years, downloading everything they said and did from age 0-7 and beyond? We are quite literally programmed to think the way we do, and we wonder why it's so hard to move beyond the stories our family have been telling ourselves for decades. Never updated, until, well, something shakes us out of it.

The collective unconscious takes up space in our minds. They say that we all have installed within us a set of universal archetypes. That are fed through us, and they come alive and wake up when we are going through crisis, acting out behaviours or going through healing. Most of the time, we are so unaware of them because they have been normalised by society. Quite often they are far from 'normal' and are feeding us beliefs and thoughts that, if we really thought about it, wouldn't be a voice we'd choose to listen to. Yet they're there, having a full on committee meeting right in our heads.

Our shadow likes to take up space inside our thoughts. We will talk more on this later, but let's just for now know; within us there are parts of us that we don't know exist, or that we are aware of but have shoved them down so far that if they want to be heard they need to shout and scream. And by gosh, they do. In our heads- in our reactions, in our triggers. But we don't recognise them for what they are. Until they are heard and integrated, they are going to keep on trying to run the show.

Our traumas are in there too. Much of our survival mechanism is quite literally geared up to remind us of things that are dangerous to us. This was very handy back when we were foraging for food, but it's quite unlikely that you will discover a delicious looking poisonous berry in the aisle of your local market. So, our nervous system is tracking for danger and is consistently listing all of the things that could lead to impending doom. That little voice can be quite convincing- it is its job, after all.

All of this isn't even considering the other factors- energetic echoes that have been left in a space that we walk right into, where someone has left a big energy behind and we are picking it up; or the random conversation that you overheard in the park; or the ego mind who just LOVES to tell you all the opinions of why you aren't good enough, clever enough or strong enough to do this, that or the other; or goes round judging the world and what it's doing that is just atrocious and we should be casting our stones right into their houses.

What if, perhaps, we could create a mind that- were we to walk in a field of mirrors- instead of glass houses- that all that would reflect back to us would be beautiful and natural, a field of infinite possibilities? How different would life be then?

So, you see, dear reader, it is not always as easy to simply change your thoughts to change your life. There are about another 14847493 issues at play here. But that doesn't mean that it is impossible. It starts with one thing…

Awareness.

Can you, as I did, make a commitment right here? Will you, as I still endeavour to every day, make the commitment to notice those voices and those thoughts? Hear them, yes. Listen to them, sure, but not take them on as the *truth*. Remember that just because you're thinking it, first of all doesn't mean it is yours, and secondly doesn't mean it's true.

Notice where your mind wants to take you. If it's down a rabbit hole you don't want to journey down today, simply notice, say thank you and ask this question…

Are you leading me towards my highest purpose?

If the answer is yes, then continue right ahead; if the answer is no, then perhaps you can choose to think again.

Thoughts + What? = Things

Have you considered that everything that ever was, was once a thought? From the building that you are in, or the chair upon which you sit- once thought up by someone who then went on to make a plan, design the architecture, source the materials and the labour, and then go ahead and actually get the thing built, to the book you are reading which was once just an idea, which formed into words which has now been made physical and found its way to your hands.

You can even think about what led you to read these very pages. Was it an idea that you wanted something new to read or from a conversation you were having with another? Whatever it was, it started with a thought.

The Law of Attraction works along with the other laws of the Universe. Through my years of working with it, I can say that it definitely is a Universal truth. Yet, it doesn't work how we often think it works, every time.

And I will tell you why.

Because, yes, it is true- everything starts with a thought- yet everything continues with an action. AND there is the very important consideration of vibration, frequency, consistency and emotion that all play a role even bigger than your thoughts.

So, let's put it this way.

Imagine that you decide one day that you are going to be rich beyond your wildest dreams! Hurrah, you have started this with a thought. Out comes Google- *'How to manifest $100,000,000'* and up pops all the TikTok's and the *'Say this to make your first million'*. So, there you are in front of the mirror stating, *"I am rich. I am abundant. Money is overflowing in my life. I am a millionaire. I am a money magnet."*

And maybe, for that moment, you have managed to get yourself up and excite those senses. Then you look around you and the bills are there, the tatty edges of the wallpaper staring you in the face, or that thing that you so want when you can afford it of course, seems so very far away. So, the next day you get up again and repeat the affirmation. But the energy doesn't feel the same. You kind of feel you are lying to yourself. The energy is off.

What message is the Universe actually getting? Well, for the moment when the affirmation is good and energised, you are actually sending out missiles into the Universe, stating exactly what it is that you want.

5 minutes well spent I say.

However, if for 23 hours and 55 minutes you are then feeling in lack, telling yourself you can't afford this, or walking around with those money beliefs that so many of us have been holding our whole lives (compounded by your ancestral line btw), you can perhaps begin to understand why the moolah isn't flying through your letterbox.

You see, it is true that thoughts become things. What you consistently think of you will notice appear more frequently in your life. When we add the all-important ingredients of energy-how we feel; coupled by action- well, that is when miracles really start to appear.

I think back to countless moments in my life where what I focused on came true; each one was due to the thought, the consistency, the dominant energy, and what action I have taken. The only exceptions have been a few of the mini miracles, which I take as some light encouragement from the Universe.

For example, the time when I was sitting in the back of a car on a long journey in a state of curious contemplation, when I said in my head,

"If I truly do create my own reality, then this cloudy foggy sky can go blue."

I imagined in vivid detail the bluest of skies and, within 2 minutes, by some incredible, jaw dropping force of something, the sky had gone from pure grey to the most brilliant and brightest blue sky I had ever seen.

Now you can imagine my delight, although I wished I had said something to the rest of the car so that they could revel in my astonishment too. We went on to find the perfect picnic spot by the lake, a perfectly placed picnic table, and in the sunshine to boot (as envisaged), with just me instructing the driver to go left, right, left.

How many of us, for example, have put a wish out into the Universe; had an inspired idea and not taken it, not followed it through, put it down to coincidence, or felt that familiar fear which stops us from moving forward?

You see, I have learned something after years of consciously working with the Law of Attraction; that it has a purpose way bigger than getting us what we *think* we want in life. Way deeper than a tool to manifest a desire or an object, and way broader than simply allowing whatever is rolling around in our heads to become the reality of our existence.

For me, the Law of Attraction helped me understand why bad things can happen to good people. It helped me to make sense of the fact that family lines, communities, and whole groups of people find themselves repeating the same situation over and over again. It helped me to find compassion for why people say things, intend things even, yet find they are unable to break themselves out of a cycle.

If our thoughts become things, and what we think we attract- then every time we have a thought, another of the same frequency will find its way to us much easier. And if we believe something, wherever we turn, we will see evidence of that very thing that isn't serving us, for the Universe is literally conspired to prove to us what we already know.

And no, it's not as easy as simply saying an affirmation in front of the mirror. Yes, it helps, and I tell you, dear reader, that this is one way of using this Universal Law- a path that requires dedication and mindfulness- yet there is so much more going on.

I wouldn't want you disheartened when things don't work out.

Remember that cheque I wrote for $1000,000 from the Universe? Despite me looking at it every day, despite my affirmations of *I am a money magnet*, despite my reading into everything I could around how to manifest, how to think and grow rich- the big win never came! Does this mean I don't believe? No, I do believe. I do believe that my heart's desires, plus the action I take, plus the emotions I have around this, plus the energy I put in may bring this to me, *if* and when it lines up with all my other desires and beliefs,

Like when that voice of our parents saying,
"Money doesn't grow on trees" or *"Money is the root of all evil"* or *"Money is hard to come by"* has been installed in by well-meaning family, by the programming of our culture and by the belief systems we hold, are finally neutralised and healed.

Like when the belief that time = money is secondary, because for me, time is my biggest commodity, and I wouldn't want to give up much more of it just to make a few more bucks.

Like when the drive to support my life and be self-sufficient is satisfied enough that I don't have to keep on expanding myself in the ways I have done in the years since I wrote the cheque to myself back in 2008- most definitely to bring me different ways to expand

Because- in my whole truth- I am glad that $1000,000 didn't manifest 2 weeks after I wrote the cheque. Because then where would I be? What would I have learned? What growth would I have had? Would you even be reading these words if I had?

So, you see, sometimes the wishes are not your true desires. Whatever that is most dominant for you will shape your life. Who knows, maybe the cheque is winging its way over somehow- but that isn't the point. The point now is to find and follow the nuggets that are leading me to my heart's true desires, heal the aspects that are keeping me separate from them, and to keep course correcting.

Over, and over again.

Until maybe even that doesn't even matter anymore.

Living With The Magic

I had work, I had time, and I had a newfound knowledge of this seemingly magical ingredient that I can create what I wanted, and it would magically show up for me. Who knew what a journey ahead it would be to get me to where I wanted to go.

If you had asked me then what my ideal job was, I would have answered,

"Being a presenter on Top Gear." For those of you not in the know, *Top Gear* is a car magazine TV show aired on the BBC by 3 men- one of whom I had an inappropriate old man crush on. *Don't judge me.*

Why was this my ideal job? Travelling, driving nice cars, well paid, being known for something that I loved to do, showing off my car knowledge and, most importantly, having an absolute blast on set- at least that was how I perceived it. Plus, the lead, Jeremy Clarkson, was one of the highest paid presenters on the BBC at that time, so who was I to say no to that?

And you know what? I *kind of* manifested it. I actually appeared on *Top Gear* twice, firstly, guessing the time the featured car, a TVR Sagaris (I remember because it was so similar to my maiden name), went round the track to within half a second of my guess, to which Jeremy asked me if I was psychic (to which I replied I am The Stig! IYKYK)! Maybe it was Jeremy that was psychic, or perhaps he himself put a thought in motion, as years later I was working in the realm of psychics myself. I thought appearing on Top Gear was my first step towards manifesting my dream. It turns out this was really true; it just looked a whole heap different to how I thought it would. *But I digress.*

New job and new knowledge. The whole world at my feet. I was progressing up through the company, I was talking at prestigious places in front of small crowds, I was learning and growing, and my Reiki practice was developing nicely.

The natural next step for me was to move on to my Reiki Two. This is the second level of Reiki which actually qualifies you as a practitioner. By this time, I was pretty obsessed with Reiki. I would Reiki almost everything from my food to the fuel in my car- really anything I could get my hands on. I could feel it flow and I knew it worked, and so back to my Reiki teacher for the next level.

It was then I discovered another miracle. Apparently, one can 'send' Reiki to any space, to any time, to anyone, just with the power of intention accompanied by this beautiful, and rather intricate Japanese symbol. I was presented with these calligraphy style Japanese Kanji's that each had a purpose, or intention. By drawing them and saying their names, I invoked the energy of power, of balance and of no time and no space.

I remember the first time I used them, meditated with them, and drew them. I could feel a distinction between them. The power of symbols made sense to me. Having studied Marketing at University, I knew too well the power a little squiggle could invoke in someone (just think about those 2 big golden arches and what they invoke in you). Didn't it make sense that if all the other Reiki practitioners in the world are using this symbol and saying this name for a specific purpose, that these symbols would hold an energy that can bring more healing or a focused intention to something?

Yet one of them didn't really make much sense to me- the distance symbol.

It's not that I didn't believe my teacher, it's just my brain didn't understand how this could possibly work. Although it did seem to kind of fit in with what I was reading in some of the Law of Attraction texts. Maybe it was another of these placebo type things? That someone would say Reiki was on its way, and so the recipient would naturally relax… but across time? Across space? Across dimensions? I wasn't so sure.

At work, some of the old patterns I was exhibiting in the car showroom were starting to reappear. Putting in more hours, skipping lunch here and there, working late and the thing with my bosses seemed to follow me into this new space. (Obviously it was them, not me, right?).

We just couldn't really get on. Everything I did wasn't good enough. I was convinced she hated me, and she was always giving me a hard time. I had progressed upwards in the company and so had she. We were both young, ambitious, competent… but something didn't quite click.

Often times, I felt set up. One day I returned to my desk to find a calendar entry in my diary. No explanation, just a meeting placed with my boss and her boss. I knew- my whole body knew; this meant trouble. I took myself out for a walk and started to work myself up.

"Sh*t, what have I done wrong? What is this about? Am I going to get fired? She's setting me up. This is going to end badly. You stupid girl, what have you done? They're going to finally realise that I don't know what I am doing, and they shouldn't have promoted me in the first place." Yada, yada, yada.

But something made me check myself. I noticed I was walking with my hands crossed over my body, with my shoulders hunched and jaw clenched, and my breathing was shallow. Hardly a posture conducive to a favourable outcome.

I remembered my training: my language affects my emotions, my body affects my language. I also remembered my Law of Attraction books. And I also thought to myself,

"Well, this is a great time to try out this no time, no space thing that I had just learned in the Reiki training."

So, I stopped, and I shook myself out. I breathed the beautiful fresh country air. I looked at the trees. I stepped into some gratitude for the nurturing, safe surroundings. I grounded into my body. I then drew to the best of my memory the Kanji for the Reiki distance symbol and said its name three times. I imagined Reiki filling the room that the meeting was to be held in. I imagined this nurturing energy washing over me as soon as I entered the room. I put the balance symbol on my throat, and asked that only truth be spoken, and that we all stay balanced during the meeting.

I visualised me sitting there calmly, and I had one clear extra intent- '*I will walk out of this meeting better than when I went in*'. I walked back through the long drive, into the building and into this pit, surrendering to what would be.

Now I need to say this is not so like me, for I was taught to prepare. I was taught to have an answer. I wanted to know everything and ask everyone their opinions. But there was no time, and really there was no one to ask. So, I did the only thing I really could do and put into practice all of these concepts I was learning. As I walked into the small library, I confirmed instantly that my instincts were right. My two bosses were sitting there, stony faced, clipboard in hand and ready for an altercation. My stomach flipped, yet somehow; I remained centred when I sat down.

The meeting started with a number of accusations, none of which were founded, or at least they were exaggerated. It was weird because as the words were flowing towards me, it was as if the energy- the venom behind the words- dissipated before they got to me. I let them say their piece, without the need to interrupt and defend myself (who is this chick?, I was used to thinking on my feet and having the answer to *everything*). And I responded. Not re-acted, responded.

I said how I felt. I got a little upset as the emotion that I had held onto for so long started to release. You see, I was always proud of doing a good job. I wanted to be the best. My Virgo rising always pushing me to be a perfectionist, yet my Pisces sun giving the impression that I find everything a breeze and that I don't really try (*familiar story anyone?*).

I also shared some of the conversations (i.e.., threats) that my line manager and I had shared, to which our boss was surprised to hear. Our boss saw with her own eyes my passion for wanting to do a good job. She understood the pressures I was working under and the undermining remarks that were often thrown my way. We got a lot out in the open, which for months had been simmering under the surface.

It was a little like relationship counselling for us all. Whatever the outcome, I felt sure I had walked out of that space better than when I went in. And they had; a different side of me revealed, a confidence within myself arose that previously eluded me.

Maybe there was something to this no time, no space philosophy after all!

The Hips Don't Lie

Now I was supercharging everything!

My manifestations were all coupled with the Reiki Power symbol. Each of my car journeys (and the brand new, white, BMW Convertible that I had just manifested) all received the power of Reiki. I was clearing traffic jams reminiscent of Moses parting the sea, I was changing the weather, I was stirring the symbols into my food, my bathwater and my bed. I was sending Reiki to world situations, football matches, and to anyone who asked. I even managed to book the one and only table for six in the coveted *'The Fat Duck'* (the number one restaurant in the world at that time), on a Sunday, on my first try- a feat which was nay on impossible, as my colleague kept on telling me for weeks before.

I should have got a bumper sticker that read *'Powered by Reiki'*.

The real magic though was the first time I sent Distant Healing.

My Nana had a life partner Bryan, who was another Grandad to me. He was in hospital having a hip operation and was having a really hard time with it. One afternoon, after getting home from work, I thought I would tune in and send him some healing energy. Sitting on my bed, I imagined him in the hospital. I sent Reiki to his hip, and then to the rest of his body. My mind was focused on sending the healing and I kept hearing in my head,
"It's okay, the doctors know what they are doing. It is okay to trust them and let them in; they're only trying to help."

I then got so dizzy that I needed to lie down and rest it off.

I called my Nana a little later, and asked after him. She told me, *"He is okay. He's recovering from the operation now, but he is feeling really dizzy.* (Oh, that is interesting). *But there has been some miracle! The doctor came in earlier and Bryan's attitude towards the whole staff has completely changed. He actually apologised for being so dismissive with them. He said he understood that they are only trying to help and that he would listen to them more from now on."*

Now, you can imagine my disbelief, my shock, my awe and my *What the*?

I said to Nana, *"Oh, wow, I have been sending him Reiki, it sounds like it has helped."*
"I wondered if you had", she said proudly. *"Maybe you could carry on? It seems to be working!"*

It turns out that this Reiki symbol truly is a bridge to time, to space, and to people. It seemed to me that it wasn't just one way, and I wondered if this was a psychic experience. It had happened whilst I had been giving Reiki before. For example, receiving the image of a dog on a lead when I was working with my first ever client, who confirmed to me that her dog had indeed tugged her shoulder on a walk that last week, and it had been hurting since. A remembrance of a particular park I had been to years ago popped in my mind whilst with another client, who confirmed that that was where he went when he needed to clear his head. A feeling of eating too much bread in my stomach with a client who had been suffering from IBS.

I was intrigued, as you can imagine- this felt way beyond anything I could make up. In fact, this felt like magic.

The Field

There is an invisible field of energy that connects all there is. We hear the term *we are all one*, but for most of us it doesn't make sense. For I mean; I am here, you are there. I am having my own experience and you are having yours. We can even both be in the same room, having the same external occurrence, yet our inner experience can be totally and completely different.

Yet we all breathe the same air. I inhale, you exhale. We all drink the same water- the same water that was also drunk by our ancestors. We are all made up of the same elements. Yet our experience, our interpretation, our involvements are all so vastly different.

There is the invisible world- this energy if you like- that circulates all around us. Some of us seem to have conscious access to it and an ability to receive and interpret the codes that are held there. I don't know about you, but I was fascinated with the psychics and the oracles that were shown to me in the media growing up. I wondered how on Earth they got their information. As I learned more, I began to wonder if actually what these psychics by the seaside were actually doing was using the Law of Attraction and the power of the mind to lead people into believing, thus leading them to experience the prophecies they were sharing.

It turns out that it is a bit of both. In fact, there is no separation between these two seemingly separate phenomena, for we are constantly both giving and receiving into this invisible field.

Firstly, through our aura- our invisible energy body that holds all the emotions, memories and frequencies in its different layers- and then out into the larger collective field.

When we are living, experiencing and actioning, we are in constant communication with this field, changing the vibrational quality of this in every single moment. We put it out, and something of similar resonance- something that harmonises with this that matches the frequency we are on- comes back to us and informs us. This continues on and on. It explains to me why so many of us can have a similar experience with something and perhaps why a small collective of people can pick up on future major events. It shows me why we all have a different internal experience because the communication channel- the receiver- can be so vastly different.

You can think of ourselves as radio receivers. Everything that we tune in to is contained in just one field. Throughout the invisible world, there are numerous channels of music, talk radio, infomercials, podcasts- all there at any one time. When one person creates a particular piece of music or records a particular podcast, it adds to this invisible field- and then depending on what you dial into, what you search for, what you are interested in- depends which part of this field we receive. Sometimes we can accidentally dial into a channel that we have never experienced before, seemingly by chance, yet we often find ourselves searching for that same familiar station or presenter that we know and love, or tuning in only to the preset stations that we have dialled into our favourites.

But sometimes, we find ourselves somewhere new. Maybe we are out of town or fancy a change, and we start to surf through the radio stations for something that we like. Everything may sound like it is another language or is unfamiliar to our ears. So, we either choose to turn it off- because unfamiliarity is sometimes uncomfortable- or we find something and try it on for size. How magical it is to find something that feels so good to tune into, or that changes our perspective or soothes our soul, that we never would have found if we had stayed right there doing what we have always done?

Funny story- there was a time I had just finished Reiki training and my car tuned itself to a radio station called *Angel*. There was no music coming out of it, but it stayed tuned to the channel for the whole ride home. I have never found this radio station again!

So perhaps every time we have a thought, this thought (and the string that then follows on and follows on- let's call this a timeline), gets thrown out there. If we stay tuned into this thought, then we will receive the information- the music- the frequency back to us. But if we tune into something else, change the dial or shut ourselves off- then we will receive something else entirely. It doesn't mean it has gone away, it just means it isn't in our awareness field anymore.

When we are using something like Reiki, or directed intention, we are consciously creating this bridge between us and someone else. We are then flooding them with a healing intention and creating this timeline for them in that moment. Holding them as healed and whole. They then receive this possibility and, as long as it matches their frequency (so they are dialled in), then they can magnetise this into their auric field and create the conditions for wellness.

A gifted healer who is open to the information, may then pick up the resistance or the circumstances that the recipient may be putting out in their field, that is stopping or blocking this route to wellness. This may come as psychic images or feelings, which the recipient can then work through- or with- to bring down the higher timeline of healing and health.

Imagine that! Does this explain the placebo effect? Does this explain how visualisation works? And why it doesn't work? Does this explain why we keep on experiencing the same thing over and over again- until we don't and then suddenly things change and continue to compound?

And how do we consciously change what we are dialled into and what we are putting out there so that we can not only receive what it is we want to receive, but also understand the infinite possibilities that are available to us? Even when right now we have no awareness that this thing is even a thing?

How can we truly know what we are destined for if the world seems to be conspiring to keep us where we are?

If we are so comfortable where we are right now, so used to the music that is filling our space, what would ever compel us to go searching for more?

The Great Discomfort

The few years that followed were a bit of a whirlwind. My first child, Max, came into the world on his due date- which unsurprisingly contained 11's in it; a number that had been following us around for years. (I got married on the 11th, he was born on the 11th, in 2011, and I was seeing 11.11 almost everywhere I turned). Work had become quite unfulfilling. I was moving up the ladder but finding that compression even harder. After a years maternity leave, I was due to go back to work just before my son turned one, but a set of circumstances that felt very unfortunate and overwhelming at the time, led me to leave the company altogether.

I had big plans, in my head at least. I was loving being at home being a mum, yet things felt intense, and I was feeling a little lost and directionless. I was missing the adult company and so found myself immersed in more books. I continued with my Reiki Training, having taken Reiki Master the year before, I found Seichem and Karuna Reiki- each one dialling me to another and another level. I retook my NLP training and took my first official Hypnotherapy course. I lost myself in novels and trash TV (yet I learned how to *smeyes* thanks to Tyra Banks). Submerged in motherhood, I was losing my identity and craving for more.

Two and a half years later, my second son Kai was born. Mum of two now, I launched myself into the role of Super-Mum. Baking, throwing parties, taking them to this and that club. I often wondered who I was and where the ambitious and quick-witted girl had gone who was now using all her creative wit to make up songs about changing nappies and getting dressed, and how her life seemed to revolve around the digestive cycle of a child.

The depth that I had so often got lost in was still there. I read all the parenting books and now wanted to know it all about how to be the perfect mother, yet feeling like I was failing badly at the same time. So much of what I read felt like it was taking me away from what I thought I knew, which left me even more down and confused.

My soul was craving freedom. My body was craving rest. My mind was craving stimulation. Yet there was no time for any of that. My boys were my life and, whilst I loved the freedom of not having to work for someone else, I felt I had no freedom at all. It felt like it should have been so easy. But inside I was ready to burst.

I would talk the talk on our rare nights out and our mini breaks we took with my mum and stepdad Steve. There was something about being away that opened something up for me and I would say how one day I will have a practice, coaching others, training maybe, giving Reiki… every holiday, every night out- the same conversation, again and again. Nothing much changed though, which I realised as I heard myself after a couple of glasses of wine, on one particular sea-side holiday, and my husband's supportive look which screamed at me, *"I've heard this one before."*

Within this all, on a regular Tuesday when my mum came to babysit, I had built a small number of Reiki clients, and even bagged a spot in an office in London giving Reiki to the employees. Those moments were everything to me. To earn money doing something I loved was like a dream come true. I wanted more, I just had no idea how to get it.

The Circle

Blocked ears and coughs weren't unfamiliar with me. Where I had in the past had to walk into the doctor's surgery to help relieve my ear pain, I had once received Reiki during a blocked ear spat, when my ears miraculously opened up and a heap of wax came out. This time I decided to go and find someone who could use the Hopi ear candles.

A new shop had opened in a town down the road. They sold little crystals and cutesy signs on the wall, as well as offering massage and readings. They had a slot available, so I booked in with one of the therapists, Kim.

During the treatment, we were talking about Reiki and that I practice it. At this point of my journey, I had recently discovered many of the Hay House crew- including Louise Hay and her miraculous work on the emotions and body connection. I was open to the fact that this blocked ear meant there was something that perhaps I wasn't listening to, when Kim casually mentioned that her colleague Pauline held a psychic circle once a week.

Something in me responded. One night a week entirely for me, talking with people who got this thing- being able to explore and discover. To talk to actual adults about things deeper than a child's eating habits and the latest episode of *Peppa Pig*. I was nervous, very nervous. I was half expecting to turn up to this coven with a scary woman complete with scarf, crystal ball and black lipstick in an incense filled room.

That Wednesday I showed up, paid my fiver and made myself comfy on one of the cute hand-decorated wooden chairs. I think my one said *Wisdom* on the back.

Surprisingly, the rest of the group seemed pretty normal. A few around my age, no incense burning, mainly women. Everyone had brought a photograph (apart from me), and we were given the task to connect psychically with the person (who was still living) on the picture.

This wasn't something I had done before. I was sceptical as to the validity of this- yet also intrigued as to what might come out. I was paired with a lady who had a picture of a young man. I clearly looked nervous and Pauline, the tutor (no scarf, no pointed hat, just a big smile and warm demeanour) said to me,

"Don't worry, do your best. Just say what comes into mind and go from there."

So, I did exactly that. There was nothing to lose really (apart from face), and no one had any expectations of me, so I started talking. We had instruction to be open to the relationship, any memories, their name and any other significant information that may arise,

"Ummmm...He seems like a nice man, quite funny- up for a joke." She nods kindly. *"Maybe he's your uncle? Or you have known him a long time because I have a feeling of you sharing jokes with him as a child. Hampshire? And the name David."*
"YES! His name is David!"
"For real?"
"YES!"

I think Hampshire was Kent, and he was an older cousin not an uncle, but it was close! Woah there, tiger! Could it be? Some of the others in the circle looked at me. *Who is this girl?* My hairs stood on end. I also hoped that this didn't single me out as the one that everyone will hate (that old chestnut coming up for review again!). *Wow.*

"Will you come again next week?"
"Just try and stop me!"

This was the start of something so deep and profound.

I had found a community. Lifelong friends. We shared, we joked, we laughed- and we practiced psychic and mediumship skills; two things I never really thought would be accessible to me. Week after week, proving to myself that there was indeed life after life, that psychics aren't all charlatans, and that there was a distinct possibility that I was psychic. I was getting better and better and I knew that this was something that had the potential to change the world- my world at least.

Connecting with Spirit was something else. Pauline was a medium at heart and would push and encourage us to go on stage and practice platform mediumship. Such great training, and so daunting. Yet, the weekly practice had shown me that the Spirit world is there, and it is my job to allow myself to tune in.

We learned to '*sit in the power*'- raising our energy vibration to open the communication channels with the Spirit World. For me, it appeared as a corridor with little doors. Someone would come through and, as soon as I started to speak, messages and memories would become imprinted into me. Sometimes they were visions, which I started to rely on. Sometimes things came out of my mouth before I even had a chance to know what I was saying. I soon learned that the best thing to do was to speak and hope. The more the energy flowed through the power of my voice, the more information came through me.

I learned the difference between Mediumship and Psychic work. That being a Psychic wasn't about predicting the future, but about being able to receive and interpret messages from someone's auric field about what just had been happening, or what had happened in their lives in the past. I understood that, from that information, we would sometimes be able to predict future timelines, expecting what may begin to come into fruition.

Mediumship was different. A medium connects to a past loved one- a spirit body- and receives messages and evidence of memories and experiences of their life past, as well as the often realisation that they are still watching over their loved ones.

Different skills using the same senses- our internal vision, hearing, feelings and knowings. The receiver still in conscious lucid awareness. No crooked nose and no scary prophecies. Just love, hope and faith in this world that is bigger than us. Of life after life.

This circle, and my friends I met within, did more for me than I think they will ever know. I felt so safe in this space. I realised who I was. I understood myself better than ever before. And whilst I still doubted myself, it was as if I had a cheerleading squad who encouraged me to continue in my exploration.

I had indeed changed my frequency, changed my zone of awareness, and changed my perception of the world, and so this began to open up more and more. I couldn't rely on my logic anymore. I began to rely on something else.

It seemed to me that it was my intention that set the course of my outcome in more ways than I was conscious of at the time.

That was when I found the Angels.

The Angelic

Angels were always a bit of a turn off for me. I would see the drawings of these little cherubs flying around the sky. Cupid and his arrow, little bottoms shining with these cutesy faces, or a more modern take of them- these blonde Californian girls hanging out with their mermaid friends and riding unicorns.

They didn't really make any sense to me.

Yet, the more I was doing this spiritual work, the more I was aware of this presence that was around me. It felt protective. I could kind of connect with it like I could in my mediumship nights, but it felt so different, and it didn't give me factual evidence-based information. Instead, it gave me encouragement and filled me with love. It felt a little more like Reiki than spirit, but it also felt different to Reiki because it wasn't like it channelled through me; it seemed to be near me. In fact, there were many times when I was bringing through messages through mediumship that made so much sense, that held so much healing, that had people crying (in a good way) because of the love that had poured out of the words that were being transmitted, yet we couldn't identify the person; it wasn't their Aunt or their Grandparent or anyone they knew- but the message was so on point there's no way I could be making it up. I had thought I was doing it 'wrong', I know now this presence was the Angels.

I found some books, but nothing really resonated. And then one day, I was listening to something, and it suggested that Angels talk to you in different ways. One was through numbers (which started off my love affair with 'sacred scribe numbers' as probably my number one Google search), but they also used electronics, other people, and the radio.

I loved the idea of divine synchronicity. That someone could be having a conversation in a café and that your Angel could just turn your head or turn up the volume at just the right time so that you catch a snippet of a conversation that is just what you needed to hear.

On my way out the door that particular morning, I inquired in my mind;

"I wonder if Angels really can speak to you through the radio?"

I am driving along, minding my own business and the car radio for some reason was dialled to Magic FM. I was more accustomed to Classic FM by this point (a parenting book told me to listen to it whilst I was pregnant to help the developing baby, and it turned out I enjoyed it). Stopped at the traffic lights just about to enter the motorway, I find myself singing along to a song I hadn't heard in a long, long time:

A song that repeats, over and over and over again, that I must, indeed be talking to an Angel. Annie Lennox, thank you. because, if I didn't believe before, there was no way I couldn't believe it now!

There you have it reader, if you find you are ever wondering the same thing, well then; Yes, Angels can indeed talk to you through the radio!

I now had a new fascination. Now the Angels seemed to be everywhere I looked. They turned up in my dreams and I would see reference to them *everywhere*. I began to understand the multitude of Angels that were available to us. From the parking

Angels to the teaching Angels, to the healing Angels, to the Archangels, and, most importantly of all, our Guardian Angel.

Imagine this- that all of us (*even you*), have a being of pure light whose sole / Soul purpose is just us. That they are assigned to you from birth, and not just your physical birth, but the birth of your *Soul* to be there for you. There is nothing else they need to do, nowhere else they need to be, no other assignments or distractions- just you. And as soon as you call on them, ask them to be there or open up to their energy, they are there in a flash.

They love you so much. They love you so much that they won't interfere or tell you what to do, but they will guide you with love and honour. Supporting you through your Soul's journey. Keeping you safe, holding you in love. Their only limitation is your free will, which they would never, ever cross (unless you were in grave danger before your time, where they have been known to step in). They know you so well. They have been with you through lifetimes, and despite (or perhaps because) being with you and knowing the very depths of you, they hold no judgement or opinion.

As soon as I discovered this, that thing that happened in my mediumship classes began to ramp up. I would be on platform, connecting with spirit, and I would start to get these accurate messages come through, yet the person couldn't be identified.

"Maybe it's a guide", I would say.

But that wasn't the purpose of these classes. We were to make sure we had someone identifiable, and we were being trained to provide verifiable, bonafide evidence. This was not that, and my curiosity needed to find somewhere to explore this further.

When The Student Is Ready The Teacher Appears.

How or when I first discovered who would become my next mentor, I am not entirely sure. It may have been Hay House Radio which I had discovered after reading and exploring the works of Wayne Dyer and Esther Hicks, but one day I hear this young Scottish guy talking about Angels in a way that I can relate to.

Beings of Pure Light. An Angel for Everyone. There for You. No Judgement. Beings of Love… He had an Angel Deck called *'Angel Prayers'* and I checked out the images. Young, sexy, cool, diverse, and accessible. Kyle Gray was just like the Angels which he so wonderfully depicted in his oracle decks and his explanations.

A short while after listening to and following this guy on his social media, Kyle starts to speak about this online membership community- The Angel Tribe. I had no idea this is what I was searching for, so I pulled some tarot cards- which I was by now becoming more adept with- and asked for guidance.

'The World' with a picture of Archangel Michael appears: Spiritual Growth. Coming Full Circle. I knew enough about the Tarot that this was a good sign. Containing all of the elements, impacting the world. Three times I asked, three times I got the same card. This was the first time I was going to seriously invest

in my spiritual growth that wasn't a certificated course, an in-person workshop or have any clear outcome.

The first call with Kyle and the 500-ish other members of Angel Tribe (Now Angel Team) was wonderful. I still remember it. I dropped all my barriers to my own greatness. My teachings in the past were to shield myself, to open up and close down, and to create an energy bubble around me in case the heebie-jeebies come on in. And here we were, energetically combined and encouraged to drop our barriers to love, to greatness, to wholeness.

There was a whole world out there of Angels, love and guidance, and it wasn't so much about learning to connect, yet more about learning to drop the barriers of separation.

That week I had a dream.

I was flying through the sky, and I looked down and saw two beautiful male figures below me. I swooped down and started to speak with them. I recognised one of them as Archangel Michael. Then, his companion, this very hot looking Angel, kissed me right there on the mouth. Ever the lady that I am, after this jaw dropping kiss, I ask him his name, as it appear in writing in front of me. I sounded it out, *A-Z-Z-R-A-E-L*. I flew back off with the warm glow of the kiss all over me before I woke up.

That dream was so vivid, I remembered it in full detail when I woke up. I Googled 'Angel Azrael'. The first site I visit gives me goosebumps: '*Azrael, The Angel of Death*'.

Oh. *Ooooop*s. I have literally just dreamt that I have been kissed by the Angel of Death. Isn't that the sort of thing that happens in movies? Should I be worried?

Luckily for me, we had a live call scheduled in the Angel Tribe group. I casually explained the story and Kyle laughed a little at my fear.

"Don't worry", he told me, *"Azrael is one of my favourite Angels."* Azrael represents transitions and change, and this tells me that I am safe, to be prepared for deep spiritual change and awakening, and that it looks like wherever this will lead me to, will be higher than I could imagine.

"Cool dream", he said.

He wasn't wrong.

I diligently took part in all of the group meditations, live calls and Angel Card Mastery. Each month, a new Angel was introduced to us where I made my own connection with these different personalities. Each month, it would bring up something for me, yet I could feel that as I saw and shed these things, I was becoming more whole and more rounded. There were times where I was seeing myself through the eyes of the Angels.

This Archangelic realm was made up of these 16 or more beings- expressions of God. (Or, as Kyle described them, the heartbeat of God) I began to recognise them as not something separate to me or not something I was necessarily calling upon, but something that was rising up in me. As I was connecting with each expression of God, I was awakening that aspect of me. My inner well of protection, or forgiveness, or love, or healing, or strength. Somehow, as I allowed these beings in, dropping the barriers to knowing them, allowing them to awaken in me, I was beginning to gain the skills and the strengths that these Angels exhibited.

Many times, as these aspects began to unlock, I would catch the opposite showing up in my life. Where courage was being shrouded by fear; where strength was being weakened by doubt; where healing was being blocked by hurt; where forgiveness was being choked by hatred; or where love was being obstructed by judgement. I would love to say it was easy. I wish I could share with you that it was as easy as allowing this Angel in and all those programmings and personality traits somehow disappeared, but my journey wasn't so straight forward.

Sometimes it was hard. Sometimes it was messy. Sometimes I had to navigate myself through friendship losses, family dynamics, worth issues, and judgements, but something was holding me through it. And often, even when times were at their darkest, the light would be shining there, reminding me that I wasn't alone. That things were growing. And that sometimes it was darkest before the dawn.

The Angels became part of my daily practice. Each morning I thanked them with a simple prayer that Kyle shared in one of his very first lessons:

"Thank you Angels for reminding me of your presence."

Things started to happen. Feathers would appear on my path. Moments of peace would wash over me. I would overhear titbits that seemed to answer my questions. I wished for a full-on apparition to appear at the end of my bed, but it never happened. It still hasn't. This wasn't my gift, my way of connecting. This learning was helping me with faith and trust. This voyage was helping me become more present. This study was to help me feel more into the subtle and open up to the possibilities that lay before me.

This journey was helping me to in-still Trust, with a capital T.

Most importantly, I didn't die after being kissed by the Angel of Death *(thankfully)*, but parts of me did, and that was the beginning of a whole new life.

Our Spirit Team

We all have a Spiritual committee. A board, if you like, of different beings, from past loved ones, Ancestors to Ascended Masters, our Angels, and our Star Families, who are all working together, with us, to help us on this Earthly quest. Like the Angels, this team are dedicated to us: one (sometimes two) Guardian Angel(s) who are there for only us, one or two Spirit Guides, who are also assigned to us in our lifetime to assist with this incarnation, and a wider team- many of whom are omnipresent (they can be with many of us at once), who resonate with our life path; particularly with things we are navigating through, and those that are helping us with our healing and learning.

I love the idea that there isn't just one being that all this lands on. I love the idea also that we can create and meet this spiritual board of directors. I also learned the frustration of having a team of beings that will advise us but will in no way tell us what to do!

When I first learned of my guides, I would often shout out to the Universe,

"What should I do about this? Tell me what to do!" And often I would get this muddle of answers come flying in. Well, that's not helpful, I would think.

"Why can't you just tell me which way to go, which road to take, which is the best one for me?"

Learning to ask better questions turned out to be the key. I had decided to have a meeting with them all. I sat in meditation and took myself up to what I now know as the Spiritual Banquet Hall (doesn't it sound lavish?). I had an awareness of different energies and frequencies in my presence. I felt this extreme feeling of love and respect.

I noticed something- they were all looking at me with a kind and supportive demeanour. Not one of them was barking orders at me or giving me unsolicited advice. They were waiting for me.

"*Hello*", I said. They greeted me back almost in song. "*What is it I should be doing? Who are you all?*"

I felt held, and accepted, safe and supported, so we started a dialogue that would change how I communicated with my spirit team from then on in.

What I learned in this meeting is that they aren't here to tell me what to do; that wasn't the agreement. They were here for this reason and this reason only; both individually and collectively, they were here to support and advise me, the Human, because I am the one that is walking this path, not them. That their opinion was just that- an opinion. Granted, it was an opinion from a higher perspective than I, but it was my life I was living and not theirs. Like a good mentor, they would be there when I asked. They would gently nudge me. They would offer their opinions but would never interfere with what I 'should' be doing. They gave me a piece of advice I would never forget-

"*Don't ask what you should be doing. Ask what you need to know. Ask for another perspective. Ask for what challenges this might bring, or what resources you will need. Ask for advice on this way or that way. Ask for the experiences that you have had in the past to awaken when you need it and ask for the courage that you need to help move through. Ask for a guide to be by your side. For protection, for peace, for safety, for encouragement, for will, for wisdom, for healing. Ask and we will be here for you, helping you draw upon all you have to support in this journey that you navigate. We know it is hard. Many of us have done this before. We know that you have every single thing you need to get you to the very places you yearn to find. We are here each step of the way. Sitting here, following your path, sending you the signs, the synchronicities, the little nods and turns of the head when you need them most. Lean on us, but don't ask for us to walk your path for you. You were the one chosen to live this life you are experiencing. Know you are never alone."* .

This changed my relationship with my guides. This changed how I asked the questions that I would often have plague me in the night. This also changed how I started to build on my readings, which I was now doing more regularly in circle and with my Reiki clients. For, if I have a team and this is how they work with me, maybe this is the same for everyone else.

Be Careful What You Ask For...

My first conscious connection with a Spirit Guide, however, could have put me off for life. One afternoon, I was sitting in my garden and reading a book. It spoke of Spirit Guides and how they are always there for us- like the Angels- as long as we ask for them. It asked me to read the following statement:

"Spirit Guides, if you are there, give me a sign and make it so obvious that you are there that I will have no doubt" (or words to that effect).

Feeling brave, very naive, and not really expecting too much to happen, I stated that out loud. And then I carried on. Home alone, enjoying the afternoon sun and wondering how this would manifest- maybe a robin, or a feather, or something or nothing, I was definitely NOT expecting what happened next.

Moments later, I hear this noise that was so loud, it made both my body and my house shake. *What the...?* My heart was beating so loud, especially as the noise seemed to be coming from inside my house. I ran upstairs, and the stereo in my spare room had been turned onto its maximum volume, blaring out music so loud the whole house shook. I quickly turned it off, went into my room and sat on my bed, completely freaked out.

At this time, it was before I had kids, no one listened to music that loud in the house, and I don't even remember the last time that stereo system went on. There was zero explanation to how this could have happened.

How I wish I paid attention to the song that was on, but I was at that moment having flashbacks of all the scary spirit films I watched as a kid and wondered what I had done. Heart pounding I state:

"Don't do that again, please. I hear you; I so hear you, but please, next time make it nicer."

I am pleased to say that they listened to that request. It was a couple of weeks later when we had gone on holiday, and I said the same thing (with the caveat of *make it nice please*). I was sitting at breakfast and the spotlight over my head was going on and off. My husband pointed this out and I said, nonchalantly, *"Yes, it's just my spirit guide"*. As I said that, the light then stayed on steady. The following day, I said the same statement, and I decided to go for a little walk to the front of the ship on my own when a pod of dolphins happened to swim up (I gave them a blast of Reiki as a thank you, of course).

It turns out that these Spirit Teams we have, don't work in isolation. They work together with others on the same mission, or others in our Soul Family, hearing our missions and wanting to help something bigger.

This truly helped me to understand how these synchronistic events come together. How we meet the teachers we need at just the right time, how people come into our lives- and go. How incidents and signs seem to cross our paths. Challenges we face and solutions that automagically appear out of the blue; Maybe even they play into the role of manifesting.

But there was still something missing, another piece of the puzzle that I wasn't quite getting or understanding.

Dedication was required. A daily practice. I now had Reiki, The Angels, my Spirit Guides, Manifesting and the Law of Attraction, Mediumship and Psychic work. A wealth of books on subjects around psychology, energy, therapy, NLP, inspiration… I think I was close to something.

I was building myself a little community, with both my circle locally to me, and now an online community in Kyle Gray's Angel Team. I felt I was being guided by something, towards something, but I wasn't quite sure what.

A Synchrodipidous Moment

Something happens when you find yourself surrounded by different people; it is as if our energies begin to merge. I know they say that you are the sum of the 5 people you hang around with the most, and it occurred to me that, as I surrounded myself with more and more people who were open and interested in the Spiritual realm, that I became more confident and interested in learning more, finding more and sharing more.

I joined more communication groups and networks. I took part in online summits, where I submitted questions and sometimes even dared to give my opinion as an answer. The weeks and weeks of sitting in circle were paying off as some of the newer circle members were booking me for Reiki and mini readings or recommending me to friends.

I started a daily practice with my cards, asking each morning, *"Thank you for helping me with what I need to know today."* I would share them in my little groups and advise on what their daily card might be showing them.

In one of these beautiful online groups, I won a reading as a thank you for my participation and my questions. There were a few readings available, and I had put out to the Universe that the one that came to me will be the best one for my growth.

I am not going to lie; I was a little disappointed when it was an Astrology reading. "*I can read my own star sign*", I thought. Whilst I was in many ways a typical Pisces, there was so much about Piscean energy that just didn't make sense to me, and I wondered truly how we could simply be split into 12 different personality types when there were hundreds of different variations- just even through people I know.

But I had won, and I was excited to connect with the lady in America over Skype.

We set up the call, and I met Willa. As we were going through the chart, I was fascinated. I didn't realise there were so many aspects. Our rising sign, our moon sign, the different planets and the different houses... So much of what she was saying to me was making sense. She knew things about me that only my closest family who knew me behind closed doors would say. She saw my struggles, which friends and my wider community would have been surprised to hear. She picked up on my dualistic nature, my need for balance, my want to escape all the time, my need to be perfect, and how that fights with my tendency to want to go with the flow. She saw my ambition and my spiritual awareness.

It was like my life and the inner battles I had faced were finally brought to light. And that they weren't a fault or something to ignore- they were part of my design and something to work with. We spoke about how aspects that will be coming up in the coming weeks and months would be an opportunity for healing and growth. We spoke about the challenges that may come up and how I have tools that will awaken to help me navigate through them. She told me,

"*In September I see a huge expansion of energy. Something big is going to happen.*" I was pregnant at the time, and September would see me in start the 2nd trimester. Maybe it was that I thought.

You see, Astrology is not just about your star sign. The way the stars align on the day you were born, and how they continue to move and flow around you, have a profound influence on different aspects of our life.

Think about how the moon affects the tides and the waters of our planet. Think about how the moon may influence your behaviour. Turns out that just before the moon is full, I am on edge. It transpires that this is the phase of the moon I was born under.

Now we bring in the other planets, the other constellations, the other signs, and the 12 houses and now we have a map. Each energy, or archetype either sits happily in a house- each segment dominating a different aspect of your life like work, home, love, body, career etc, or feels uncomfortable, or has an opposing force- which may explain why you have never felt at home in your body, or talking in front of a crowd, or in a relationship. It may show why sometimes things seem to flow (the stars aligned, and it just seemed to happen), or you can't get your words out or everything you say is misinterpreted (Mercury Retrograde anyone?!).

Now I had a new tool to play with. Now I can see where my strengths lie naturally and where I need to look harder. Now I can see that I am a natural communicator and that I am being pushed to offer things in a grounded manner whilst opening to divine intervention.

Now, things were starting to make sense. Maybe this time I had spent, all this interest that I had fostered wasn't a fad. Maybe it was a sort of destiny, and maybe this was what I was meant to be doing. Maybe *my* stars are aligning, and I am actually becoming who I was born here to be. Maybe all the oppositions that show in my chart weren't a curse making me flip from one extreme to another, but a route to balance and harmony. Maybe that is what I am searching for.

Suddenly that September things started to really expand. I was getting braver and starting to run some online readings low key on my Facebook page, which had gone from 50 of my friends and family humouring me, to 500 in what seemed like a flash. I was getting some referrals too and my confidence was growing and growing.

The Angels were coming into my readings and giving me guidance through a higher perspective than that which I was receiving just working psychically. People were telling me they felt good after having these readings from me. I remembered what I had been told by Willa-

"In September, there will be an expansion."

So, I message her and tell her that her prediction was correct! That my readings and my healings were growing in both frequency and depth, and I really felt like I was getting somewhere.

I was intrigued by her reply… *"Oh, hi Melissa. I have been thinking about you since our call, and I would LOVE to read your Akashic Records. Would you like that? In return you can give me one of your tarot readings I have been seeing on your page."*

In that moment I had no idea what it was she was talking about, but my body knew otherwise and, goose-bumping in the balmy evening, I found myself replying; yes!

The Akashic Who?

The little hairs on the back of my neck stood on edge. The Akashic Records... well don't they sound mystical and magical? A quick Google search showed me that they contained past lives and held the information of all my lifetimes. *'Interesting'*, I thought. I have been looking into the possibility of past lives more recently, having read the fabulously insightful book *Journey of Souls* by Dr Michael Newton only a few months before.

OK, I am in!

I had no idea what to expect, but whatever I might have had in my mind, it wasn't this.

Willa's instruction for me was to just find somewhere comfortable, with my screen on and relax. She said a simple prayer, and I am pretty sure her voice changed ever so slightly. It was as if I could feel her in my energy field right next to mine. She asked me to tune in.

"Tell me, what is happening Melissa?"
"Wow, I just feel like I have been kicked in the chest by a horse."

That was the very first experience I had in the records. It came with no other explanation, rhetoric or storyline, just this distinct feeling that I had been kicked in the chest. How I knew it was a horse I don't know, but that was what it felt like. Since that day, I have had that same sensation twice, and I still am not one hundred percent sure on what it is or why it happens...

She waves her hands around the screen and guides me through questions, whilst I am being given this gift of having my mind filled with imagery, sensation, understanding, feeling, memory, knowing.

I am in a cold, dark and damp cell. I feel a deep sense of guilt and sadness. I am pretty angry; my belly is hungry, and I am all alone.
"How did you get there?"
I stole some bread. My family was poor, and they couldn't eat. I saw this loaf of bread on a bench at a market and I took it to feed my siblings. I got caught, and now they are going to chop off my hand. They told me I was a bad, bad person and that I had ruined their life. The words had hurt me as much as the punishment. I took on all the guilt. I believed them. And my siblings now think I have abandoned them, and I know not whether they will survive or die as I await my fate.

I could feel the guilt and shame welling up inside. It moved into anger and regret, with such guilt resting there in my hungry belly. I told myself I deserved to be punished and that I was a bad person.

Willa helped. To be sent to jail and sentenced to the loss of a hand just for stealing a loaf of bread- this is not justice! She continues to wave her hands about, blowing and I feel this wave move over my stomach and chest.

"It is ok. You are safe now."

I forgave myself in that moment for carrying what seemed to be lifetimes of guilt. I also softened the anger for the person that threw me to the lions, for I understood from that perspective that he too was scared- scared of his master who would punish him should he not account for every piece of bread on the stall.

I am on a cliff. I am being marched forever backwards. They have torches and are chanting something I cannot understand. I am scared. I am being called names, accused of hurting someone- a child or a wife of a clergyman, it is not clear. My voice is shunted. I am unable to speak as I walk backwards, up and up, seeing this mob progress towards me.

I tried to shout out- *"I haven't done anything wrong! This wasn't my fault! I was trying to collect some herbs to help the fever and saying prayers, not curses."*

They wouldn't listen; no one would. So, it didn't matter whether I spoke or not. They all wanted me dead. I was scared. I didn't want to die but knew I couldn't live with this group besieging me. I could hear prayers being shouted out by a man- were they trying to perform an exorcism? Was I being prayed over? I couldn't understand, and then, with one last shout of venom, he spat in my face, and I fell backwards, off the end of this cliff. My body bounced and crashed down and down until I surrendered to death.

Right there, in my room, my body was shaking. I felt so cold, and my legs were uncontrollable.

"What did you want to do there, Melissa?"
"I wanted to tell them what I was trying to do. I needed to share my truth."
"Tell them now Melissa, share."

And so, I imagined that happening. I imagined me standing on the edge of the cliff and shouting back *"NO!"* I heard myself telling my story, sharing what really happened, declaring my innocence, asking for a part of them to understand me. As I did so, my throat had sensations I can't describe, a clearing maybe.

They heard me, or at least it seemed. The energy of the pack seemed to soften, and then I fell backwards as a sign of surrender, trust and freedom.

I am walking up the stairs. Round and round; the stairs felt like they would keep on twisting and turning. It was hot against my bald head. This was the place that I yearned to be in, but I felt so unfulfilled, so used, so fake. These stairs just spiralled round and round; they never ended. Up and down, down and up. How long had I been walking for. Days? I couldn't speak. I had taken a vow of silence. There was no one that needed to hear my words, my words were just for God. Just me and God. But I had so many questions. I had come here to learn and to grow, but I had to give up every comfort. I had to shave my head. I had to get up with the dawn and walk these steps round and round and round until nightfall and beyond.

It's a warm day and I am kneeling on a cold floor. It is more silent than I have ever experienced, with only the sound of my breath and a brushing noise. My knees ache, so does my back. I have the world's smallest brush and I am cleaning a floor which is already sparkling clean. I am sure that this is not what I signed up for. Yet there is a deep peace inside me. There is nothing else to do or be or act or know. Just me, this floor, this brush and my breath.

Clearing after clearing. Revelation after revelation. It was as if my memory bank was on full form and delivering to me images that I couldn't always describe. They made sense. They were patterns that I held, mainly subconsciously, that I hadn't ever been aware of their origin.

Why was I always betting on the underdog? Because that was me.

Why did I feel like everyone is gawping at me and judging me all the time? Literally happened.
Why was I scared to charge money for spiritual gifts? Because I had renounced my worldly goods.
Why did I want to ask all the questions, all the time? Because they were suppressed for so long.

These were questions I didn't even know I had, yet somehow, in this space and under Willa's expert guidance, I was being offered this gift of knowledge. With that awareness came the revelation that I needn't carry this anymore.

Lifetimes of guilt, shame, anger, confusion, vows, and misunderstandings were being opened up into my awareness, without the attachment to the feeling that I had left unhealed for so long.

And then Willa said, *"Find a lifetime where you were a teacher."*

I was confused. Why a teacher? What has this got to do with anything?

I am in a hot and dusty country. I am in a makeshift classroom of young children. Maybe I am in Africa somewhere, but I know that I am not from these lands. I had come from a stable and wealthy family but had decided my work was here. I had upped and left it all behind. Some of the other families in the area didn't like what I was doing- providing education to the *lower* classes. I was outcast, lonely, and oh so different from anyone else. I had made my choice and there was no going back; although really it was only a letter and some swallowed pride away should I want to.

I fast forward to later in that life. It seemed such a thankless task. The school had been closed down due to lack of funding and hate crime. I went underground so to speak and helped just a couple of orphaned children, but I was pretty destitute myself. The life felt like a waste, I had failed, they were right, and I was a misguided child that should have wound my neck in from the beginning.

Then right there in the Records, I have a vision. It was if I met, in the spirit world, one of the children who I had taught. A child who had taken the faith I had given him. The belief that, like me, he could do anything that his heart was leading to and that his heart would never lead him wrong. In this telepathic communication we had together, he showed me the difference he made in the world. What he made of himself; the people he had helped; and the thing he had invented that had gone on to assist so many people.

"Miss", he said, *"this is because of you."*

The rejoice in that moment! The relief. The acceptance that- YES!- my heart would *never* guide me wrong. I did not waste my life, I did exactly what was required of me. Sure, I could have lived a life playing croquet on the lawn, but instead I had chosen this. Despite the hurt, despite the misery, and despite the hardships, the hate and the seeming failure of my plight. I had made the world of difference to this one boy, who had gone on to make the world a better place.

And that was when I heard it.

"You are a teacher, Melissa. Now is your time."

Me? I couldn't see it. Who would I teach? What would I teach? Who would listen to me…?
"Teach right here", I hear. *"In this space, in this sacred realm. The answers are all here."*

Was I dreaming? Was this my mind playing tricks on me? Was this some grandeur complex playing out?

Willa went to close the session. I was exhausted by this time. Despite being tucked up in my warm bed, my legs were shaking uncontrollably. I didn't really know what to say. I wasn't sure what had happened. That was profound and I was speechless.

It was late by now; more than two hours had passed. Willa suggested a salt bath and bed, so I took myself in the shower and scrubbed myself down with Dead Sea Salts, letting the energy wash over me.

That night I slept and dreamt.

I was travelling places. Seeing faraway lands, moving into higher realms, and talking to faceless people. I remember being in a spaceship of sorts, seeing a control panel and being given instruction on how to operate the ship. I remember at one point saying,

"I should probably go back now, my husband may wonder where I have gone."

In that moment, I felt myself land back in my body. It was 2am, and I was pleased that I still had time to travel, dream and integrate.

Who knows where I went that night? I have wondered since if it was a form of Astral Travel. I didn't even know what that was at the time. Yet somehow, that sleep, and that experience helped me to make some sense of what had happened the night before. I awoke the next morning feeling different. Energised somehow. Lighter. A little groggy, but also clear.

Willa messaged me shortly after asking how I was. I am sure my message back was something reminiscent of a fan girl wanting to know more and gushing at how wonderful that experience was.

"We must get your reading in, Willa"- the exchange we had agreed upon. Her reply?
"Melissa, I would like you to read my Akashic Records."

Errrrrrrrrrrrrrrr...say what?

"I don't know how to do that. I wouldn't know where to start. Are you sure? What if nothing happens? I, what, me, who... I mean... how?"

Imposter syndrome came up to say hello that night. But this time I wasn't going to let it stop me.

Reading the Records

Have I mentioned I am a spiritual geek? I, of course, already had 3 books on order to help me understand the Akashic Records, past life and healing. She recommended the works of Linda Howe, who had a pathway prayer that would easily get me in the records. So, we set up the meeting, with little time to prepare, and she encouraged me saying,

"Let's just see what happens."

The night came. I was nervous as anything but also excited. I had with me my favourite card deck (*The Archangel Power Tarot* by Radleigh Valentine) and I had printed off the prayer. Willa was so kind and supportive of me. *"Don't worry"*, she said, *"we will ask some questions and you can just discover what happens."*

Now, usually when I do readings, I would use the cards and then I would get some extra information from the Angels or the guides in the form of quick visions, symbols or knowings that I would piece together to create the story. Images on the cards would stand out for me and give me metaphor and answers to the questions that they had. When Willa asked me to help her understand a particular relationship, I asked the question, and I was straight away taken to a scene on a boat. It was like I was in a 4k 3D cinema. I could feel the lapping of the boat, the emotions of the people and, as I spoke of what I experienced, the scene moved forwards.

"We are on a boat. The sea is getting rough, and you and this other person are on it. You need to make a choice, as there is too much weight on the boat. Either keep the thing that is the lucky

charm or talisman, the spiritual artefact if you like, or keep the goods that you are to deliver to make the money. You both have a different opinion. She wants to throw over the energetically precious and keep the monetary precious, and you are the other way round. Things got heated. She threw the talisman overboard, which seemed to anger the sea. As you had felt, this led to the boat toppling and neither survived."

"YES!" She said, *"This is the dynamic that is happening. I understand now why she behaves the way she does, and why I feel I cannot trust her in that way!"*

Let's look at this one now.

There are two brothers. They went out hunting, and the younger sister was left at home. The two brothers were keen, quick triggered, liked to tease and were also deeply protective of their sister. This particular day, the sister was begging to come with them, but they knew it wasn't safe and that she wasn't capable of getting the job done. However, she had other ideas and decided to follow them. She was hiding in the bushes and, as she moved to get a better look at what they are doing, one brother saw the rustling in the bushes and shot. When he realised what he has done, he ran to her rescue, carrying her with the arrow in her small chest. He screamed, he should have known, he should have trusted her, he should have been firmer. Should, should, should. He repeated, "I am sorry, I am sorry. I am sorry."

Willa's face said all I needed to know. There was indeed a third person involved in their story, and once again she confirmed with me that this is very reminiscent of what was playing out in their relationship at the time. It brought to her compassion for the young girl who still wanted to 'come out and play' whilst the two friends in this case had more 'serious work to do', and why they always felt to give in.

Me? I was in absolute awe of the way these messages and these stories were literally downloading into my head. How the words tumbled out. How the cards were reflecting what I was seeing, but I didn't need them; the information was coming through. Even though I couldn't provide 'evidence' like I had been taught in my mediumship training, the evidence was in the resonance and the understanding of the resemblance of this time and that.

This was not a coincidence. This was deep and I felt at home in this very special space. But what actually is this space and how does it work?

Miss curious brain set herself on a mission to find out.

The Akashic Records

Have you ever wondered where your thoughts come from? Why you show up in the way you do, with your quirks and your gifts? Why certain spaces or places, religions, archetypes or personalities really draw or repel you? Have you wondered what drives you, and what holds you back?

Of course, there isn't just one reason. We are a product of compounding energies and experiences that build and build over time. Yet sometimes we are unaware as to how much time that has actually taken.

Perhaps you can be open to the understanding that somewhere there is this field of energy- this energetic holding space that contains everything that has ever been thought, said, done, actioned. Every feeling, every story, every experience that ever was, and ever will be, held in a library of sorts- or how I experience it- an energetic superhighway of information. Much like the internet, there are billions of thoughts, ideas, pictures, graphics and symbols. Once they have been submitted, they are there- somewhere in internet land- forever.

This space is known as the Akashic Records. A Sacred space that houses all of this information. Each of us has our own record, which comprises of everything that us, as a Soul- us as an incarnate being- has ever known. Nothing gets missed out. It is all there.

I often think of those court transcribers whose job is to record every word that gets spoken. Imagine we had a team of these typing away, not just what we say, but how we feel, what we think, and how we behave.

This library therefore contains all of our experiences from this life and lives past. A wealth of information, this space is accessed through our vibrationary alignment and our intention. Held by a group of beings, the Akashic Librarians and Guardians if you like, to ensure the integrity, the privacy and the sanctification of the space.

All of the experiences that you have had holds an influence to some degree. Now, if you can think about just how many thoughts, feelings, ideas, intrusions and actions you have taken just in the last minute, hour or day, you can imagine that this space is dense with information.

However, my experience is not of density. My experience is that when you enter this space, you are immediately connected with this expansive nature of unconditional love, non-judgement, and understanding. This space feels like home, because truly it is. This space where you stand in limitless potential, with the capacity to learn those programmes, behaviours and experiences that hold you in limitation through this life. Plus, the possibility to know and activate the resources you have within to move you through whatever it is that faces you in this lifetime.

The Akashic Records have the ability to help free you from your past and take you into the boundless possibilities that await you.

I believe and have experienced that, if our intention and vibrationary alignment is right, we all have the opportunity to access these records in a conscious way. The truth for me is, many of us access the records unconsciously in times throughout our day.

Maybe when a memory pops into our brain, it is due to this alignment retrieving this record and presenting it to you. Perhaps when a solution to a problem we have been facing drops down, we are pulling upon a resource that we had stored in our records. It could be that when we have an idea, that some greater force has aligned our unique set of circumstances with a solution to an issue that has been called upon by someone else.

You see, our Akashic Records are not an island. Our personal records are ours, held and accessed only by us and those we give permission to. Yet they all form part of a wider field. The Akashic Realm connects humanity- in fact, it connects all Souls together. Understanding the impact we have upon each other. Helping us find solutions and connections to help us to grow and heal. We all play our part, and if we could see this field with our eyes, perhaps we would see this beautiful light show of resonance, connection, and withdrawal. A pushing and pulling of energies, a coming together and a moving apart like a dance. Some records lighting up and shining bright in a different array of colours and shapes, which touch and move others to help them light up, move or shake.

Our actions, you see, are never just about us. We are all connected and, whilst we have our own individual viewpoints and experiences, we are indeed all part of one large consciousness.

And it is the Akashic Records that documents it all.

The potential held in this superhighway of information is far reaching. Far from being static, in this realm we can bring healing or understanding. We can voice our truth and learn and grow. We can bring change to ourselves, and because of its infinite connected nature, this spills into our relationships and circumstances, manifesting into our reality.

Which is one of the reasons why it is so important that we respect this space. That we enter in gratitude and in truth of who we are and what we need. That we enter with the intention of the highest good for self, and for all those that are connected to us. That we do this for the betterment of self, of us and of all.

The more one explores and delves into this space, the more we get to know about the infinite potential that is held through working in this field. I couldn't have known in that time how much this discovery would change me, would influence me, or would inspire me. But it did in ways beyond what even I could possibly attribute.

The Path of the Teacher

The weeks that followed my initial discovery of the records seemed to flow. I had by this point been attuned to Reiki for around 8 years and practiced every day. The principles of *just for today* were becoming more embodied. I looked back and understood that now I did worry less. Anger played less of a role in my life, and I was certainly more grateful and kind- even to myself.

Being initiated into 3 different forms of Reiki, I had the experience and the knowledge to talk about Reiki all day, every day (and often I did).

So, going about my life, reading more into the Akashic Records, continuing with my psychic development and launching more into the online communities, in 3 separate conversations I was asked by 3 different people if I knew another Reiki Master called Mel in the area.

I didn't but, knowing that there is no such thing as coincidence, I had to now find out who this woman was. So, I looked her up, and she so happened to be running a Reiki Teacher course- which had a space become available. Now was that time.

I was so excited to be taking this course. It had been a while since my attunements and so a while since I had been immersed in a weekend of Reiki. To learn how to pass on this wonderful system; to empower others to bring healing to themselves and others; and to gain access to new understandings and new ways of doing things was incredible.

One aspect of the course was to bring a presentation to the group to help us develop our speaking skills and to learn how to hold the space of the class. I chose the subject of how our mind and our thoughts heal our body. I spoke with a freedom and confidence that I had not experienced before. I felt safe in the moment. I felt like I had something important to say and, for the first time ever, I didn't feel like I was being judged and in danger of being humiliated in public.

A shift had occurred. And now I was finally a qualified Usui Reiki Teacher. I figured I had time on my side as I was 7 months pregnant and decided that now I had some time to write my course materials, start to put a plan together, and maybe start this teaching thing sometime later next year (or three).

But the Universe, as it does, seemed to have other plans. One of the girls in my circle contacted me.

"Melissa", she said, *"I want to learn Reiki. And I want you to teach it to me."* I think I tried to talk her out of it, even recommend someone else, but she was adamant it was to be me. I pointed to my growing belly, and she nodded and said,
"Yes, so we will need to do it soon."

6 weeks later, I had my first Reiki student. My course material was written, my class agenda done, the space set and she turned up to learn.

What an experience this was! To teach, to share- I came alive! I loved every single moment. To watch someone grow ignited something in me that felt exciting, natural and magical. It was like the Reiki flowed through in a way I had not experienced before. My pregnant belly was flipping around in joy as my unborn child also received the benefits of this healing life affirming energy.

I was a Reiki Teacher; I had claimed it. I looked back to just a few weeks before, a time that now seemed alien, a time before I had even considered becoming a teacher. Willa was right- this is who I was.

As soon as I claimed it, stepped into the role, and accepted that YES, this is right, the path continued to evolve. As I discussed with others about my interest in the Akashic Records, and this utter sense of awe I had with the information that came through during that first session with Willa, the questions, the interest and the volunteers came along. So, there I had a plethora of other human beings who wanted me(!) to go into their records and see what they found out.

Then, Pauline, my circle leader invited me to demonstrate in the circle. *"How about you read mine?"*, she said. Not only that, but also to do it in front of the rest of the group. I said yes before I even knew what I was doing. There was something a whole lot bigger than me compelling me to do so. Plus, I was very pregnant, and this magic baby inside me had seemed to be a good luck charm, enhancing my psychic abilities and spiritual connection one hundred-fold.

The next week she asked me something that hadn't been asked of me before:

"I am booked on a demonstration next week, and I wondered if you would mind taking the circle for me?" The rest of the group seemed genuinely excited by it. *"OOO! Can you share with us what you know about the Akashic Records?"*

I had a whole week to prepare. Each night for the last month at least I had been diving into my own records, repairing the pillars as outlined in Linda Howe's book. I was getting quite adept at opening mine, and already starting to experience the power that seemed to be held in this space. So, I upped my game. I wrote a class schedule and some notes. I poured everything I had learned over the past few weeks into a handout and turned up the following week.

As I sat there, my insides were flipping. I had all these faces looking at me, and I started my presentation. My face was burning hot; I am pretty sure I looked like a beetroot. My voice may well have been quivering. I was hoping the words would come out right; that I was doing this beautiful subject justice. I led them through a two-hour workshop, and everyone had an experience. Afterwards, everyone was gushing.

"I really enjoyed that."
"You are such a natural".
"That was awesome."
"Can you run another?"

I was floored. I was flattered of course, but I felt inside like an imposter. I passed all the learning and the enjoyment on due to the simple fact that the subject was so fascinating. I was convinced that the only reason anyone said anything about how good it was, could only have been because they were my friends.

However, I kept getting asked. I was asked to run the class at least once a month as Pauline got more and more busy with her mediumship demonstrations. She trusted me with the group, and the group trusted me with their energy.

Only a few days after running that workshop, I got a call,
"Hi, I heard you know about the Akashic Records. I would love to meet and have a chat."

So, this stranger, who I don't even know how we came into each other's world, came to my house, to be greeted by me and my huge pregnant belly. We spoke about spirituality and the Akashic Records. She asked me questions and the answers appeared from somewhere. We hit it off and then she came out with it.

"I think we should run a workshop together. I have a group of women who would be interested, and I have a venue already. I know you are the perfect person to do this. And we will teach people how to read the Akashic Records."

It had been 16 weeks or so since I first discovered the records. 16 weeks since I had heard the message in my my own records that I am a teacher and that I am at home in that space. 10 weeks since becoming a Reiki Teacher. Maybe 4 weeks since I ran my first circle. I started to politely decline. Once again, pointing to this pregnant belly.

"I am due in 2 weeks, so we can look at starting something in the summer?."

"No, it needs to be March. If we start in March, that is our biggest chance of success." She was a numerologist. She was also a wonderful salesperson. And I really, really liked her. Her belief in me was somewhat contagious.

"You realise I will have a 4-week-old baby in March?"
"That is no problem, you can bring him along!"

I could see that there was no getting out of it. Besides, this seemed somehow fated.
"I'll whip up a flyer", she said. Before I knew it, the course was set, and people were booking on. I thought maybe 5 people; how wrong was I? On the first of the 10 workshops, 15 people had turned up. More than half of them had committed to the full 10 weeks.

I was now with a brand-new son, this little miracle of an Angel. He had already been to circle with me at 2 weeks old (I wanted to test if my increased psychic ability had disappeared now that I wasn't growing another human inside me- I am pleased to say it hadn't), and had come strapped to me during a practice public mediumship demonstration that I just didn't want to miss. He was a pretty chill Reiki baby (remember, he had been there during my master teacher training, and received, by default, the master attunement, as well as been present during my first ever passing of the Reiki system). So yes, he was chill, and quite happy snuggled in this little hammock of a sling I wore.

So, there we were, and the fateful date in March rolled in. I arranged my mini suitcase of prep work, paraphernalia and shop items I had accumulated and turned up, feeling very ill prepared (*I could not have prepared more even if I had a year*).

I remember turning up in the room, cleansing the space, filling it with Reiki, creating an altar and saying my prayers. I don't think I had ever called so hard on the Angels to be with me.

"Thank you", I said. *"Thank you, Archangel Metatron for being with me and overseeing this workshop. For assisting me and the group in safety and with love, accessing their Akashic Records. Thank you, Archangel Gabriel, for watching over me, for helping me find the words to speak, for assisting in making the conversations flow and for talking through me when I do not know what to say. Thank you, Archangel Raphael, for bringing healing to this space. For assisting all that attend so that they may heal and grow and be filled with love. May this workshop be a success. May all enjoy it thoroughly, and please Angels, please, let me come out of here having done the very best I can (and don't let me make a fool of myself)."*

Fifteen faces stared back at me, many of them strangers. I was scared as life itself. Yet, when I started, I surrendered. I surrendered somehow to the energies that I knew were here to support us. I felt this wash of calm come over me. The words flowed. The healing happened. The time went. And I heard those magic words at the end of the night-

"Thank you, Melissa. Can't wait till next week."

And so, it began.

The Imposter

Let's talk about imposter syndrome.
It is an actual phenomenon, and I would put bets on that the very best in the world have experienced it. And if they haven't, well, I am not sure if it is a case of good for them then, or actually a symptom of another syndrome all together.

I have experienced it time after time. Usually when the highest expectations are put on me (usually by myself), or when (and here is the clincher), it is something that I am deeply passionate about and want to get the message out there.

How does it show up? As a fear that one will be exposed of as a fraud. That people will 'find out' that we don't know what we are talking about after all. Where we doubt our skills, or our talents, and even our accomplishments, and think that we are no way qualified to be sharing, holding or even talking about this thing.

Oh, and there are so many ways it can materialise. The *I need to do one more course* syndrome. The *I am going to spend hours and hours preparing notes* syndrome. The *I will quote everyone else's ideas instead of my own* syndrome. The *I am feeling sick, the moon is wrong, Mercury is in Retrograde, or I got a bad feeling thing that makes us stay at home rather than showing up in full force* syndrome. The *insert any excuse you want, however viable or outlandish and hope they let me off* syndrome.

Over the years it has shown up- and I suspect will continue to show up in all its different guises. It is quite clever really, how it tries to convince us that we are indeed right about our fears- and that yes, it is best left to someone more clever, more experienced, more psychic, more prepared- or at least more 'not us'.

But you know what I have discovered? That it is just a voice. It is just an opinion. And more often than not, it is just trying to keep us safe. Safe from making a fool of ourselves. Safe from stepping too far out of our comfort zones, and even safe from harming anyone else. And I will give it some more credit. Often, it is based on something that has really happened. Maybe something that happened 4 lifetimes ago, or perhaps something you witnessed in a movie, or even when a friend at high school called you out and shamed you for sharing an opinion that had no backing.

However, what I have learned is this- this opinion should be taken as just that. If (or should I say when) it shows up, rather than let it hold you back, just ask yourself: *"Is there anything else I really need to know or do to be better prepared for this? Is there really a gap in knowledge or am I just procrastinating? Do I know enough to be able to make a positive difference to this audience? And do I care enough to get it right?"*

Now these answers may not always be satisfied one hundred percent, and that is OK. Your imposter syndrome is truly showing you that you care about what you are about to do, and when you treat it as an opinion- rather than as fact- it can become a whole lot more manageable to deal with.

Be prepared. Be passionate. Practice if that helps, but know that just because the feeling of, *I am not good enough* presents to you, it doesn't mean it is true.

The truth for me is this- if I listened to it every time it showed up, I would probably be hiding somewhere in a corner, rocking to the sound of my breathing. You certainly wouldn't be reading these words. You care, and that is a great thing. You want to do your best, and that is also a great thing. So be brave, have courage and take a little step. You may be surprised as to the gratitude and impact you make for stepping where many wouldn't dare. Besides, if you don't, it may well be that someone way less qualified, and way less passionate but a bit braver, steps where you wouldn't dare, *and you wouldn't truly want that, would you?*

The morning I was due to be delivering my largest group of Reiki Practitioner training, I wasn't feeling so good. I hoped it was just the early morning start and the getting up with one of the kids through the night. I got through the first day of training fine. However, as soon as the last person packed up their things and walked out the door, my throat did that thing that I was oh so familiar with. As a teen I used to get tonsillitis, and that feeling of my throat closing up and my head feeling full came over me full throttle.

I went home, had some soup and went to bed. All through the night, I was wondering how on Earth I would deliver another day's training if I couldn't even speak, let alone feeling like I did. In a funny turn of coincidence, one of the students had ordered some Neal's Yard Remedies products from me, including throat capsules, soothing throat spray and elderberry syrup. She insisted, when I turned up the next morning that I dosed myself up on her new hoard of goodness, which I did. By some miracle, I felt well, and the course ended with a group of happy, well equipped Reiki practitioners.

Over the course of the next couple of days, something miraculous began to occur. I have never healed from tonsillitis so quickly. At school I was easily thrown off for a week. This was on and off for a few days. But then something strange happened-the next time I was running Reiki training, I got that same feeling in my throat. I woke up and couldn't speak. This was familiar I thought, drank some healing tea and went on my way.

After the third time I found myself with a sore throat and without a voice when I was about to deliver Reiki training, I figured something must be up. Is this my guidance team telling me to leave it, that this wasn't my path and that I shouldn't be teaching Reiki?

That didn't feel right. I loved sharing this system, and I loved even more the power that was being created in my students, who seemed to love the training. But I don't believe in coincidence, and this was a coincidence too big. So, one evening, I decided to take myself into a quiet space and explore in the best way I knew how.

I entered my Akashic Records with this question in mind- *"Thank you for revealing to me the origin of this symptom, and what I need to know about healing it."*

I was shown a series of images flashing in front of my eyes. It was a little like something out of an old-fashioned horror movie or a nightmare; though whilst I was witnessing this, I wasn't at all scared. I could feel the fear of the woman I was perceiving– me, a long time ago. I could hear echoes of shouting, of pleading. I was aware of accusations being thrown upon me.

I could see a hangman's noose.
I saw a town square.
I saw a trial.
I felt the resignation.

I flashed once again to the scene on the cliff I had experienced in my first session in the Akash. I saw a version of me lecturing to a crowd, and then the cold sensation of being harnessed to a guillotine.

I experienced all of this in just a moment, and all with curiosity, empathy, and understanding. I was aware of the fear, the blame, and the shame. This was real. I placed my hand gently upon my throat and felt the surge of Reiki energy flowing through my hands. I knew what to do. Drawing the distance symbol in my mind, I sent Reiki via my throat to each of those versions of me. I heard myself forgiving the perpetrators. I recited Ho'oponopono, an ancient Hawaiian prayer over and over-
"I am sorry, please forgive me, thank you, I love you". I felt I was saying it to myself more than anyone else.

My throat started to close up a little more, and it felt as if this honey-like liquid was moving through it. An Archangel appeared. I knew him as Jeremiel, cloaked in black, beaming a honey-coloured light through the opening of the hood. I saw him in the faces of all those that were haunting this memory.

"I am safe". This was in my own voice now. Reassuring my throat that it is OK. It is OK to speak. It is OK to be heard. It is OK to spread this message of power.

I thanked my throat for trying to save me and my body for doing its best for remembering what had happened to me in lives past, that had proved to me that sharing my message wasn't safe. My body doing what it was designed to do- keep me safe. It needed that reassurance, that knowing, that yes, I acknowledge what happened, I accept that this was how it was, but *now* things are different. Now things are safe. In fact, I had never been safer than now.

I spent time letting the healing occur. I placed a crystal- Lapis Lazuli- behind my neck as I lay down, and another- Blue Lace

Agate- on the front. I must have drifted in and out of a restless sleep as I allowed the healing to take place.

When I woke the next morning, I noticed something. I had always had this thing where no one (not even me) could touch my collar bone. It made me retract, feel sick even. Now I could touch it and there was no recoil... I wondered if I had healed what was there.

It was all revealed in the next few Reiki trainings and the Reiki shares I held. Before the session, I would feel the feeling of a dry or scratchy throat- never as intense as I had before, but still there. I took the time, I gave myself some Reiki as it came up, and I reminded myself of my safety. I said thank you for reminding me how much I care about myself, thanking my body for alerting me to this perceived danger, and reminded my body that this was an old echo and that now, together, we were safe.

I created a new pattern. I wrote a new record. Acknowledging, being aware, healing and the reassurance was what was needed to update the server to its latest setting.

Does it ever come up again? Yes, not just with Reiki, but when I am about to launch something big, when I am about to step out into something new, share a new message, or help people claim their power. Sometimes it comes up, and I do the same thing. I honour this part of me that is scared, assure it that I will do all that we need to keep safe and well, and I thank it for reminding me how powerful this next experience will be.

I learned that this was a feeling that reminded me how much I care, and how much impact this message is likely to have. It reminded me to take care. To be prepared. To allow myself to be heard. And it reminded me too how this message was ready to be heard by people that wanted and needed to hear it.

The Fear of Being Seen

Could it be, when something is so deeply ingrained in the collective consciousness, in our own minds and DNA, it could ever go away? How can this ever be healed? I asked my guides, and this is what they told me.

"So much of the day is spent seeking outside. Outside for validation, outside for confirmation, outside for distraction, outside for the answers, outside for reassurance. We put so much trust in other people- authority figures, gurus, mentors, the TV. Even our dreams and our guidance we receive from beings outside of ourselves. No wonder we cannot trust what we have to say. No wonder we cannot trust how we show up."

The more we rely on external validation, the less we know ourselves. And, if we are unsure of who and what we are, and how and why we serve, then we understand that our actions and our words can have such a profound influence on others, we become scared to put a foot wrong.

Truth is, that part of the fear we feel, is that we care so much about others. We see the polished version of this or that theory, or their lives, or how they do things, and our messy, often unexplainable, and sometimes very simple thoughts do not seem to match up to what we expect of others.

But people need people; we all need each other. And we need each other to show up as our full selves. Because then we have all of the notes in a chord, or all of the colours in the spectrum- not competing but playing together in harmony.

It is when we either try to be another note that our sound comes out too flat or too sharp. Or when we are not in tune enough with what our true harmonic is, that we do not know when to come in, when to play with others, and when to sit there poised and ready.

So, we first get to know which note we are, and which key we are most comfortable in, and then we fine tune by bringing healing, practice and awareness to self. We allow our note to be the clearest most vibrant version of itself. We understand where we are, and that we- like every other note on the keyboard- have a place. When we are in flow, we play a beautiful harmonic.

Sometimes, we fall out of key. Sometimes- either through neglect, an environmental condition, or through the need of a general tune up- we do become out of tune. We can still play of course, but our attention must go back to what we need now. How we sound against others, if we are still in the same key, or if we need stretching more. Or even if it is time we moved to a whole new instrument.

This journey is not a straight line. This is a symphony, a harmony, a whole concerto of notes. And you are key to that. You found your place right here in order to play and be heard. Know yourself first, then seek to become the best version of you. But don't stop playing until you find her, for she is there- you just sometimes need to understand where you are.

Of course, this does not mean that you stay static. That note that you are can be played on many different instruments, in a cacophony of symphonies, in a variety of keys. Sometimes, something happens where we seem to have changed from a key to a string to a beat... and that's ok. We are evolving after all, yet here, in this moment, know who it is you area, find your particular note, how you resonate, how you sound, the range that you hold and commit that you will play it to the best of your abilities, continuing to fine tune and know its nuances for as long as it is resonate for you

And so, this began how the guides spoke with me. Through healing words and metaphor, through encouragement, and through my own voice and writing. Not outside of me. Not something I was reaching towards. Not something separate. A part of me that was always there, so long as I took the time to tune in.

Now, my job it seemed is this. Go and find out which note, in which key and which instrument I am at my most resonate.

"Universe, can you help me?"

The Shaman

Continuing my search for more, I became a bit of a workshop junky. Lucky for me, the local shop was well connected, and when I heard that there was a day workshop that was being put on around Shamanic Practices, I knew I had to be there.

I didn't know much about Shamanism at the time, but something told me there was a compelling reason to go. Despite still breastfeeding my son, and this would be the longest I had spent without him, we arranged that he would come over during the lunch break so I could feed him (more for my relief as he was always happy with a bottle). Besides, he was now a regular circle member with me and was always calm in that shop. I was looking forward to the first day to myself in a while and delving into my spiritual practice again.

As we all introduced ourselves, I proudly listed off my list of accomplishments-

"I read Tarot, the Akashic Records, work with Angels, Reiki Teacher". *Yada yada*. I saw the tutor look at me, kind of smiling with a knowing look on her face.

I forget exactly what we learned in that workshop, although I do remember being more convinced than ever that this Spirit world was not only real, but the truth of what the world was built upon, I remember the amazing tools she brought along, the rattles and drums, the totems, the items on the altar. I also remember filming the spirit activity in the room at the end of the day and being amazed. There it was, physical tangible evidence of this spirit world that had been impressing upon me for so long

The feeling I had when I left that workshop was that, it turns out, I know almost nothing. What I think I know is only a grain of sand and there are a million more things that I don't know. This was only the beginning, and I had found the lady to teach me.

I attended every single workshop she put on. Each one understanding more about my practices and my connection. Each one bringing a deeper healing. Each one understanding and experiencing more about the things I had learnt at a surface level and delving deeper into the energetics behind it. It was as if all I thought I knew was becoming more real and more tangible with each passing month.

Some beautiful synchronicities were in place. Like the day when she played the sounds of the crickets as we were connecting with the Earth. For the first time in my life, I had heard that sound whilst scrolling through YouTube that afternoon. Or exclaiming that on the way to the session it seemed the sun was emitting golden rays, when she said *"we are working with the golden light today"*. She saw I was keen, and I asked if she did private mentorship. She declined and said she worked alone.

So, I made the most of the workshops. Oh, the healing that occurred! Soul Retrieval, Ancestral Healing, Past Life Journeys, Animal Guides, Cord Removal, Cacao Ceremonies. We even had one experience where we dismembered our bodies (through a journey obviously- health and safety and all that). Fascinated, in awe, I was growing in strength, and I could feel it echo out through my life.

Then one day, I had booked for a private session. I wasn't really sure what I wanted or needed, but we did some deep work together. A short while later- maybe a year or so after we first met- she offered me private mentorship, inviting me to become her fist apprentice. She requested to pass to me the Munay-KI Rites with the idea that we would hold the ceremony together.

I don't think I even took a breath before I agreed. It felt right with every part of me, an honour and a privilege. This world-renowned Shaman (which I didn't even know she was at the time), was offering this to me. She saw something in me, and we had a connection. I was about to receive a medicine that I couldn't have anticipated its effect on me.

The Energy Of Love

The Munay Ki; 'the energy of love'. I mean, who wouldn't?!

The Munay Ki is an energetic transmission passed from the Q'ero Tribes- The Shamans of the Andes and the Amazon- and made up of nine initiation rites. They heal the wounds of the past and upgrade our DNA to re-inform it and transform our luminous energy body. By receiving the rites, we accept stewardship for this Earth and for all creation, growing into luminous beings that live, heal and die differently.

I had been offered the Munay Ki no less than three times before by three different people. For one reason or another, it didn't happen. This however was the calling I was waiting for.

She lay her hands upon me, immediately feeling this sense of being held and supported by tribes and tribes of people. I had an awareness of them all tumbling down a hill to stand behind me and beside me, as they supported me through this change.

We took the rites over a number of weeks, allowing me to connect in with their energies. The Seer's Rite awakened the ability to see the invisible world, and it did. The leaves looked more vibrant, and there were times following the transmission that I am sure I could *see* the wind blowing. The Healer's Rite awakened the healer for myself and others, and I received the Bands of Power.

The bands activate an energetic protection around you. Consisting of all of the elements, the sun and the moon, it works to harmonise and transmute all of the energy that comes in. After all, everything is made of the land, the air, the waters, and the fires, and so having these invisible bands, connected with nature- becoming nature- was allowing me to step upon this Earth as a part of this Earth. Built from the same building blocks, honouring the significance and sacredness of the Earth upon which I walked, allowed me to work with less fear, and more connection.

It was tangible too. Once a week in the mornings, I would replenish my bands as I walked down this lush little alley on the way back from taking the kids to school. I would breathe in and ask for the bands to be revived. I would push them out and send them into the lands, the seas, the fires, and the air. I would feel one with them all. And then, when times were hard, when I was walking alone, or in a highly energetic environment, I would consciously connect with my bands. I would ask them to activate and to assist me in transmuting anything that is throwing me off, alchemising it back into its original form. Bringing to it the energy of peace.

One particular day, I was on the London Underground with a new friend. It was busy and she was getting a little overwhelmed. I suggested that she pushed her aura out and created a safe space around her. She asked me how to do this, and so I activated my bands and pushed them out all around me. I explained that our energy body is all around us, and by consciously connecting in, we can manipulate our field. To imagine this light within and around and push it out far around you. In that moment. the train doors opened (Luckily, we were still stationary at the station)! We looked at each other– wow! That was both obvious and impressive. Of course, she booked onto the next workshop so she could have those bands of her own!

Knowing that the elements are with us, and that we are one with them all, reducing everything down to its essence makes everything easier to deal with. Our energy body then knows exactly what to do with it all. Without the baggage it carries or any excess, we can begin to use the energy we are subject to, to replenish rather than drain us. This was a game changer in so many ways.

The Harmony Rite was precious. Placing seven seeds within my body- one in each chakra- I remember vividly connecting in with the archetype of the animal that was being placed. The Serpent, helping me to shed my skin; the Jaguar, assisting me between worlds; the Hummingbird, bringing the sweetness and joy in my life; The Eagle, helping me to soar and rise above the storm, protecting the heart space to give and receive love more freely. The energy shifted as the energies from the three worlds, lower, middle and upper, allowed me to journey into the other realms with greater ease, connecting me with parts of me that had laid dormant for so long.

Even if the rites stopped there, it would have been a gift, yet the next three; the Day Keepers Rite, reminding me of the importance of my place in every single day that I am gifted a new dawn, and my responsibility to bring the best of me to each day; the Wisdom Keepers Rite, which connects with a lineage of wise men and women, introducing me to a new guide; a Mongolian lady who loved to talk through me in a funny accent when I was alone and often made me laugh with her blunt attitude and twinkle in her eye; and the Earth Keepers Rite, where I took on the stewardship of this Earth. The Earth that I now had responsibility for, assisted by the Earth Keepers of the past and the future, who could help me become a better citizen of our home, planet Earth. I noticed then how things changed. More mindful of my impact, my eating habits were starting to change. Fresh vegetables had never felt more appealing, and I am pretty sure my plants were responding better to me.

The last two rites- the rites of the time to come- were done on the same afternoon, which brought it all together. Receiving the transmissions- head-to-head, I could feel the energy and the wisdom pouring through me. My body was responding, and I made a connection with what I can only know as my Star family. This was the rite that informed my DNA, and I wonder if this is where the catalyst was for the upcoming changing in my body started. Followed by the Creators Rite. There is something about knowing that *we* are the Ancestors of the future. That we are, at this moment, the source of creation. That we are not just human, but we are spirit, walking as humans and embodying the spirit of the change we wish to see in this world. Agreeing and taking on responsibility of the world that is yet to come, for our children's children, generations from now.

What a gift it was. I felt different, I stood differently, and I acted differently. I wanted to share this with the world. But first it was my duty to germinate, feed the seeds and receive the guidance that was coming.

On that journey home, I asked for Jaguar to walk with me. I was feeling a little ungrounded, and felt I needed the protection of Mother Jaguar to be present. This was the archetype that intrigued me the most. So, I go to take the 15-mile journey back home in the car. As I pulled out on the main road, a black Jaguar car was driving in front of me. I smiled- not a car you see every day, and what a wonderful synchronicity! The three numbers of the number plate were 444- what are the chances of that?! I wanted to take a picture, but I was driving in moving traffic so did not think I would get the opportunity.

14 miles later, I am still following this Jaguar; almost all the way to my house. When we finally came to a complete stop, I snapped a quick picture, the lens low down in my car. When I got home and looked at it, I couldn't quite believe that the numbers on my car dashboard at the time of the picture read 1:11, and the car had been with me the whole journey, only turning off less than half a mile from my home.

"Thank you, Jaguar,", I said. *"I will never doubt that you are here by my side, whenever I ask. I am grateful for your protection and your strength. Thank you for confirming your presence to me in such a clear and beautiful way."*

I have had an affinity with the Jaguar ever since. A beautiful protective animal that often walks by my side and assists with the deep work I am sometimes called to do. She shows up in beautiful synchronistic ways every now and again, but she knows I trust she is there.

The whole experience of being given those rites, and the honour of passing them on over numerous workshops alongside my mentor was something that will always hold me. The magic that happened in those ceremonies amazed me every time, from miraculous healings to apparitions of feathers in the middle of a closed room, to the insight and the physical changes in the space. Being in that energy created such magic and insight, that each time I grew more. More in my truth, more in my ability, more in my awareness and more in my connection. Working with her was daunting for sure because I knew so little compared to her experience, but each step was another step up. And my Mongolian guide would talk me through it before each and every workshop, leaving me buoyant and full of trust at the start of every day.

The Way of the EarthKeeper

Something happens when you take stewardship of this Earth. You are given a responsibility of the land that we inhabit, understanding that every word that is spoken is either raising or lowering the energy field around you. The effect that even one person can have is pretty humbling. Creating a mindfulness and a presence within.

As you walk this Earth, it is as if you are leaving footprints behind, and you can choose if those footprints are treading light and gold into our Earth, or worry, fear or doubt.

Now, I would love to say that this particular brand of medicine- or any of the practices for that matter- breaks through all of the programming and all that has been installed within us, but it doesn't. What I found is that it made me more aware of the consequences of my actions and my behaviours, which in all honesty can be a hard pill to swallow.

Whenever I was walking without congruence, drawing upon old behaviour patterns, and doing the things I had always done, it became really uncomfortable. Looking back, it needed to really, otherwise how would I have known what needed healing? How would I have known what to change?

And so, the journey helped me to realise my sensitivity. Not to abhor it or attempt to abolish it, because I am stronger or wiser than that; but to honour it and figure out ways to work *with* it, not against it. I turned to spending time alone, replenishment, changing what I put in my body, and on my body. I became more sensitive to the onslaught of smells and chemicals around me.

Rather than curse this, I thanked my body for helping me to live better, become healthier, and for helping me to understand where I can make those small changes to compound into something better.

After all, I was one of the Earth Keepers now. A Day Keeper. A Wisdom Keeper, and I had a duty to better the planet. I had taken on that responsibility, and I had generations from the past supporting me, as well as future generations looking to me to help make the change. And you know what? The victimhood I had felt before believing '*what difference can one person make?*' had been healed, and I held the responsibility right there.

And that is not really the easy path.

Yet, there are some beautifully easy practices one can bring in, to ensure we walk these golden footprints into our Earth.

A particular favourite is the Metta meditation. A simple affirmative practice where you repeat the phrase whilst exuding kindness-

"May all beings be free from pain. May all beings be happy. May all beings experience kindness. May all beings be free and happy."

Saying this phrase, or something similar that comes to mind at least, whilst walking the street is so beautiful. I am pretty sure it is felt by the person passing- by sending the blessing their way. I have had many smiles along the street when I have simply been repeating this mantra in my mind. They surely feel it.

Often you will see me walking down the street- sometimes with the kids- dropping little orange or red berries we have picked from a passing shrub. The kids love to throw them in areas shouting,

"Have some love and blessings!"

The Metta blessings in practice - a moment during your day

- ⬦ Take a berry or something natural (little firethorns or winterberries are perfect for this) and bring your breath onto the berries with a simple affirmation of love, kindness, Metta or blessings.
- ⬦ Walk around, dropping them every now and then, knowing that all that pass this- the Earth and the land in which it stands- will receive the intention you have imparted.
- ⬦ And/Or listen to the accompanied Metta Bhavana Meditation in the resources section here: melissa-amos.com/mystics

There is the added benefit that demonstrating kindness actually releases feel good hormones in you and this joyful practice will set you up for the day ahead. And who knows, there may be an energetically sensitive being who just needs that kindness that you have sent that day!

One person really does make a difference. I wonder how that one person today can be you?

The Karmic Load

But what about all the patterning and the Karma? I am not quite sure how in one chapter I can truly explain and give this huge topic justice. What I do know is that, whilst old patterns surface sporadically, how I respond to them has changed over the years, and the frequency of them recurring has certainly diminished. Can I put that down to one particular practice, ceremony, experience or technique? I wish I could. Maybe one day we'll discover it, however for me, I have tried many of the cures, and I believe they have all compounded in one way or another.

So perhaps starting with Karma is prudent. What is it? Payback? A wrong we need to right? Inevitable? A curse?

Through my experience in the Akashic Records, on working with myself and with hundreds of other Souls, I am not sure it is any of those things. I highly doubt it was anything that was imposed upon us, but rather lessons, circumstances and experiences that somehow, we know, on a Soul level, that should we move through them, we will grow in this incarnation. We will experience something that will give us the lesson, the tool, or the understanding that will help us become closer to who we truly are- source expressed as a human.

We have heard and read it time and again: Source or God or the Divine is in all things. *All things.* Not this thing and not that because we do not find that to be wholesome or worthy, but in all. The good, the bad, the black, the white, the light, the dark, the here, the there... everywhere and in all. So surely, as we experience more of all, we become more of what we truly are. Now please do not get me wrong, I do not think we must suffer to become whole, because if we are all one, then it also stands to reason that perhaps we can also learn from the lessons and behaviours from others- tapping into the collective. It is when we truly take heed of the lesson, acknowledge it, grow from it, and become more from it, that perhaps it is then that we neutralise whatever Karma it was that we were holding.

I have often wondered where judgement falls into this. That as we judge others for their behaviour or their beliefs, that we are in the moment separating from them. That is different from me. That is not of God, and this is. Perhaps we are then in some way taking on the lesson or the karmic load that this person is also moving through. One thing I have learned about judgement is this- we really only judge what isn't healed in ourselves.

So where does that leave us? Right back to self. Right back to: where can I bring more compassion, more understanding, and more awareness into me and my behaviours? So many of them are unconscious that is often hard to tell.

Even writing this makes my mind want to explode, but truly it is simple. We do the best we can with what we know at the time. And as Maya Angelou said, *"When we know better, we do better."* When we don't, then we may begin to accumulate more lessons to move through. You see, this isn't punishment from a higher force, this is you and your Soul wanting to do better. So, we find ourselves in these circumstances, possibly behaving the way we have always behaved, because that is all we know. Moving round and round in circles. Perhaps our Soul guiding us going,

"Yes, this time she'll see it. This time he'll know it. This time they'll get it." And when we don't, it inevitably comes round

again, and so we put it down to karma. How, oh how, can we break free from this?

How? We seek to know ourselves better. We understand our mind and how it works. We bring to the forefront, one by one, everything that we carry. We are brave enough to question our beliefs, to question our superiors, to question the status quo. We allow ourselves to take a moment into lucidity, by first seeking to be aware, second by seeking to understand, and then by seeking to heal, make better, or create anew.

Karma, in my opinion, is not trying to hold you back or punish you. Karma is there to help you know where it is you are seeking growth. So that you can indeed know better, and so you therefore do better.

Maybe this is why us parents hear our parents in ourselves; to free the karmic bonds of generations. Maybe this is why new generations come in with different ideas and different harmonics, wanting to change things to a new frequency. Maybe even this is why we are so much more connected and so aware of other cultures, ways of being, viewpoints- often so different to our own, so we can hold a mirror up and go, *"Hmmmm… is this OK, just because we have always done it like this? Maybe we can do better?"* And so, as a species, we become more aware, and our Karma begins to heal and lift.

Because you know what? It only takes one person to show it is possible, and then records can keep being broken.

It only takes one. And that one can only be us.

The Cords Of The Past

It began to dawn on me, how much of me wasn't just me. How much of me was my parents, my ancestors, my bosses, my religion, my expectations, my teachers, my friends, my high school memories, and my past lives.

How could I truly know me if I couldn't differentiate between what was mine and what was an entanglement from one of the many relationships and experiences I had ever had? So, I set to work.

At first this journey was all about the external. I sought to 'cut cords' with all people and situations that no longer served me. Cutting cords is a process- often done through meditation or through the use of crystals, reiki, via a declaration, or even a ceremony, to sever the energetic ties that we hold between us and others.

In theory, it makes a lot of sense. We are energetic beings, and science has shown that once a particle has been connected to another, they can continue to influence each other across space and time. If we couple that with the complexity that we humans are- with our mind, memories and our need for community- it makes sense that we are not immune to this.

However, what I found was that, however many times I cut cords with certain influences in my life, they would continue to show up. Take one of my old bosses for example. I knew he still had an impact upon me years from when we even last had contact, as he would show up in dreams or I would hear his opinion when I was doing something. I would feel the trigger when an ex-colleague spoke about him, or even when there was the possibility of bumping into him. So, I would cut the cords and then, a short while later, there he'd be again.

It wasn't until I understood more about what these cords are and actually how they tie in (mind the pun) with quantum entanglement that things shifted. Let's put it this way- if I had a cord and you had a cord that were interlinked, and for many days, months, years- even lifetimes, we were passing energy through to each other in healthy or not so healthy ways, that cord would hold a certain vibrational frequency. We would, in some way or another, be used to this energy transfer and a pattern would have developed where we draw from or pass on nourishment, guidance, power, anger, and so on through that cord.

If we were just to seek to cut it, sever it through the middle and that be all, it doesn't take into account the resonance that has been created. The pattern that has occurred. And dare I say, perhaps even the karma that has been built. And so, whilst in the moment those cords are indeed cut right open, they are left dangling about like some Kraken, waiting to find something that it can feed off or connect to, to satisfy its need.

And so, we find another situation with a similar trait, or pattern or energetic frequency, and they connect right back up. Or we are so used to being together, that by some form of telepathy- or maybe even through the theory of quantum entanglement, we are right back where we started, thinking,

"Well, maybe it is just us."

You may however be pleased to know, there is a better way.

Cord balancing. Oh, such freedom it brought as I journeyed down into the lower world. The place that in the Shamanic worldview holds the hidden or disowned parts of ourselves, the space where our ancestors live, and the realm of the collective unconscious.

Inviting in firstly the higher selves of those that I am connected with, that are in any way draining my power, a series of beings came to my awareness. We started by removing all of the hooks from both myself and the other. Taking them from the organs, around the arms, the knives in the back, the sexual areas, the brain, the ears… one by one releasing the hooks and throwing them into the flame. Inviting in not just the energy that I know from this current incarnation, but through all experiences we had had together, and all resonate experiences that were linked. Each time we threw these into the flame, a balm came to heal us both, to tend to the wounds that were left.

I then asked for the experiences, the understanding, and the lessons to be shown to me. I saw a scene come to mind, where I had been shot in the head as some form of mercy killing by the very man that I had considered to cause my life a misery for so long. I understood from this space that he did this act out of a kindness I couldn't quite understand at the time, and I also saw his frustration of the trouble I had gotten myself into. We were on different sides of a war, and he could not protect me. Yet he saved me from a fate worse than death by causing my death. That energy imprint was hugely affecting us both. I could understand how this had started to play out in our working relationship in this lifetime. Not quite so dramatic of course, but resonance of behaviours, guilt, expectation and responsibility. In that moment, a huge forgiveness happened within me. The lessons that I had been so blind to. My defiance that was playing out again here because I refused to see his point of view, now could suddenly step down. I no longer needed him to save me, and he no longer held the guilt and responsibility of the power he had held over me in times gone.

I felt free. The dreams stopped. And I even bumped into him, and we had a very warming conversation. The cords were balanced, and the lessons learned. The body no longer needing that source of nourishment, and that karmic field no longer moving me in the directions so that I could finally see what I had just seen.

I had become more of me. And so, I repeated this exercise again and again; each time releasing more. You see, it isn't about cutting it off. It is about changing the quality of the particles so that they no longer need to be volatile, and so can vibrate in their stable, whole and healed self, no longer looking for another to create the stability that particles naturally seek.

Maybe this was where my year one Chemistry in college finally made sense!

Energy Hygiene is so important; a skill that we so often overlook.

I Call Back My Power

These journeys into the worlds of the Shamanic traditions, with the accompaniment of my Jaguar who continued to work with me, helped to shed and transmute many of the echoes of the past. I realised that, as I was carrying so many thoughts, beliefs and expectations that were not mine, that somehow, I had lost a part of me along the way.

Until that moment, I was continuing to seek that sense of fullness through other avenues. Food was a likely choice, distraction felt helpful, external validation was sought, even co-dependency tendencies would arise.

And it was in one of those trips to the lower world that I discovered a lost part of myself. A part that had been hidden for fear of not being enough, or even of being too much. A part of me that had been shut down and kept securely locked up, waiting for it to be safe enough to emerge again.

Now was that time. I saw the conditions that this part of me believed it needed to return. I became aware of the woundings it had experienced, and the reason that it didn't feel safe enough. It was like little bits of me had hidden there over lifetimes, knowing that one day I would come back for them all. Gathering them up, holding them in safety, and becoming ready to feel their power once again.

It took a little healing. It took some help from my Ancestor guides and the helper beings that were involved. It took a little guidance from my mentor, and that power returned. It came back. It seemed that, in that moment, I became ready, even if my boots were shaking, for what was next to come.

I called back my power. And I didn't want to let it go again.

Call Back Your Power - A 1 minute practice

- Hands on your hips, in the 'Wonder Woman' pose (*optional*), sitting or comfortably standing is fine.
- Imagine a force field of light around you
- State: "*I call back my power*"
- Imagine all the little filaments of you- like iron filings magnetising back to you.
- Imagine them moving through the force field of light, cleansing and activating as they return into your energy body
- State: "*I give back all that is not mine*"
- Imagine all those little filings that are not yours moving through the force field, cleansing themselves and returning back to Source or where they belong
- Repeat for as long as feels right for you
- Complete by stating: "*I am Whole, I am Sovereign, I am Free*"

Energy Hygiene

As we become more conscious of our energetic aspects, one of the kindest things we can do for ourselves is practice Energy Hygiene. We clean our bodies and our clothes. We understand about physical boundaries, yet we wonder why we end up feeling depleted, drained or anxious for no apparent reason.

I discovered that, despite the healings, the big ceremonies, and the deep journeys that I had experienced, it was quite easy to lose your power again. To get sucked into everyday life. To give away your inner you for what you are told is right or necessary. To be out and about and in the thick of things, and to come home feeling depleted. To make promises or agreements when you know it isn't aligned to you, but you didn't have the heart to say no. To run on empty and not listen to take the time you need to replenish. To be in these energetically intense environments- crowded places, rallies, public transport, concerts- and be influenced by all that is around you.

Of course, that is normal. We didn't choose this lifetime to sit on top of a mountain to reach enlightenment. That is the easy life (and I wonder how many of us had that training over other centuries). *This* is the real world, and maybe this is part of our training. To learn to stay centred, grounded and in our power, regardless of the circumstances that are going on around you.

This is not about hiding away. This is about claiming and commanding your energy. This is *your* energy after all!

So, I developed a practice. It has evolved and changed over the years, but the essence to it is this. We begin by cleaning and clearing. This can be a physical body brushing, or through a visualisation, or even through a spray or smoke cleanse if you have the time. It needn't be anything fancy, and you needn't have any special tools for this. In fact, it is best if you don't because this little practice needs to be available to you wherever you are.

So, you clean and clear. You then look to upgrade- to bring the glow if you like. This can be accessed through a spiritual retreat space such as the 12D Plasma Field or the Violet Flame, or through gratitude or kindness. The key here is to find yourself something that will raise your vibration to a level that can only magnetise miracles to you. Think of something or someone you love or are grateful for and let that energy course through your body.

You then use this energy to create a forcefield around you. I am not one anymore for shrouding a cloak around me- after all, I didn't incarnate to be hidden this time. Whilst sometimes an energetic cloak is exactly what you need, it is important to know that these cloaks or bubbles are indeed available to you when you need them. But I digress. Using this upgraded auric field to become a forcefield of light, to inform your very cells of the power and the love that is available to you, is, in my experience, a far superior way of keeping your energy where you want it than any other I have found.

One statement that I found so life changing- brought into my awareness by the 12D Platinum shield- was this simple declaration:

"My declaration of intention is to serve my source. I commit to serving my highest power, wholly, fully and completely. I am free,

I am free, I am free." (Inspired by the Energetic Synthesis version of the 12D platinum shield)

What a life changer. Connecting me with my highest self; my source. Acknowledging my highest power and letting that lead the way. Declaring that this is what I connect with and no other, made it clear to me and my energy field where to focus my attention. Intention is everything, and this was a powerful one.

It is as if this intention connects me up to source, and down to Gaia, as well as surrounding me with light. It is adaptable to the situation, and leaves me open to guidance, but to the only thing that truly and fully has my best Soul interests at heart. My highest version of me. It hasn't failed me yet, and I continue to say this statement and share it with my clients for years after practicing it.

The homo-luminous energy body I had committed to develop was developing more and more. As this all became lighter, it often took more care. Regular energy cleansing through salt baths, physical therapy, and one of my favourites- an energy spray, which I could walk through its mist after any particularly heavy days.

Clean your energy like you would look after your physical body and you can't go wrong. Nowadays, a great boost for me is a cold shower (after a hot one of course), which seems to boost my inner circulatory, after cleansing myself and imagining any energetic debris falling off me in my warm shower, accompanied by essential oils.

If you take just one thing from reading these words, it's this: your energy is your responsibility. Get to know it, look after it, and know it will lead where you direct it, so begin taking charge today.

The 12D Platinum Shield - 10 minute practice

- The 12D platinum shield was introduced to me by a mentor some years ago. It is an energetic retreat space that connects in with the 12th Dimensional Light that is available on this Earth, which connects to you through your platinum Merkaba Star.

- To connect with this, envisage a platinum star filled with living light in the centre of your brain. Drop it down your body, through the Earth and into the very centre, where you will find the Platinum Earth Star. Fill up from there, charging your energy body with the little light filaments.

- You can then create a force field around you with this platinum light by bringing your star back up to your Earth Star (12 inches below your feet), creating a foundation and a pillar around you.

- Continue to bring the star up through your body, filling you with the light filaments, out the top of your head and into your Soul Star, 3 feet above you.

- Seal the light in with another field above you, and then send the star up to the centre of the Universe - to your Evolution Team, your highest self and your cosmic guides to watch over you and ground multidimensionally.

For a free version of this recording, head over to https://melissa-amos.com/mystics or visit Energetic Synthesis 12D

The Pylon

Being sensitive to energy can often leave you feeling battered, and so many people drawn to this work are energetic sensitives. I have learned that this is indeed a superpower, but one that needs to be honoured and kept in check.

Knowing my energy cycles, I have learned what can lead to burnout (often the hard way), and what is nourishing from my Soul. Sometimes I just need quiet. Sometimes quiet leads me down a rabbit hole that is not affirming to go down, so sometimes I need action and to be busy.

I had had enough of being in spaces, or even of doing readings and then coming home absolutely floored. I would feel like all the energy had been zapped out of me, or so heavy that I had literally taken on the world. So, I asked for guidance. I wanted to be sensitive, for this is what made me good at reading energy. It helped me to receive information, to help heal others, and to do what was fast becoming my full-time job. As they often did, the guides offered me more metaphor and guidance.

I was shown a huge telegraph pole, with wires and electricity running through it. I tuned in and realised that this image was representative of me. It showed me in a very simple way that in any situation I could be one of two things- a receiver or a transmitter.

If I was receiving, then it was super important that I was connected to the right source of energy. My highest self; the Angelic; the support of the Divine; the highest selves and guidance teams of my clients; the Reiki energy; and Source. I was then safe to receive and bring that energy through my body.

Sometimes, of course, a stray wire would get in, or sometimes I would need to plug into a situation that was calling for my attention. At that time, I can switch in order to receive what I need, and then turn my circuit on to transmit. So, I am receiving from above and below me, grounded in (like all good electrical circuits should be), reaching up to the highest heights and standing tall. Yet now I am transmitting this energy- me the conduit and making a difference.

I can always switch, to read the room or check for environmental change, the key, was to be conscious of this, and where the energy is coming from.

Maybe in reality it wasn't as clean as that, but it made complete sense to me. And so, when I next took a trip to London on a busy Christmas weekend, I tested the theory. It was intense and I felt it. I found myself being thrown off a little. I was getting overwhelmed and impatient. This was not me, and this did not feel good. But I noticed, and rather than go down the usual habit of taking it out on those closest to me, I switched my focus. I imagined I was that pole, grounded deep into the ground and connected to the energy that will support me. Asking that to fuel me, I then turned on to transmit.

I endeavoured to become the highest frequency in the space because doesn't energy follow energy, and doesn't the highest frequency become dominant? I was transmitting light, love, and strength. And it all changed, for me anyway. And perhaps it was because I was walking around with a strange glow about me, but I seemed to have a little more space along my path. Kindness seemed to find me, as a compassionate stranger helped us navigate the buggy down the crowded staircase.

Something worked, it was simple; yet it required a mindfulness that wasn't always easy to hold on to. Yet the more we do it, the more we create those pathways and those habits. Noticing when you are pulled and when you are swayed. Grounding multidimensionally as a habit as usual as brushing your teeth, so at least you start off on the right foot. And then keep on noticing until it just becomes your normal.

Next time you are in that situation dear reader, perhaps you can remember the very uninspiring image of a telegraph pole and allow it to change your input and output settings.

Need a boost? - try this 2 minute practice

- Wherever you are, ground for a short moment into your breath. Hand on your heart or your belly, tell yourself:
  "I am safe right here".
- If it helps (and you're in appropriate surroundings), try body brushing, shaking or tapping the body to help release.
- Feel your feet on the ground, and imagine a spinning, drilling energy spiral moving the base of your spine/bottom of your feet deep into the heart of the Earth. Allow your excess energy to drain into the Earth
- On an in-breath, pull up that depth of nurturing Earth energy, and then invite in a higher power and ask for it to watch over you, protect you and keep you safe.
- Declare: "*I am grounded Multidimensionally into the Earth and the Heart of the Cosmos. I draw my energy solely (Soul-ley) from here.*"
- Then, if you feel up to it, you can then imagine that light beaming all the way from your heart space, all the way around the perimeter of your surroundings, as you continue to draw in, and now share the energy around.
- Say to yourself: "*I am free I am free I am free.*"

What Is My Purpose?

So many answers to this question, it blows my mind even wondering where to start. I had heard about purpose, read books on purpose, even attended lectures on the topic- but the answers of joy and satisfaction, and on growth and paying back karma– well, they didn't really cut it for me. I figured that I'll find out for myself from the best source I know- Source!

Entering into the Akashic Records that day was much like the other days. I went into my sacred holding and allowed for the energy to swirl around me, feeling that feeling of unconditional love and support that comes with being in that beautiful space. That day, I didn't really have any personal questions or deep healing to embark on, and I was in a contemplative mood.

As the guides approached me, the wise looking wizard-archetypal with long white hair and matching long flowing white beard, complete with the standard uniform of the pointed hat, warm smile and glint in his eye, showed up almost riding on a cloud. I greeted him and we sat on the sofa that I had led clients to many a time.

"What is the purpose of this life anyway?" I asked. *"I know to grow, to have joy, I know to right wrongs, and to connect with people, but I see so much suffering, and things are so hard, and joy isn't always accessible for everyone. What about children born in extreme poverty, or in war conditions? What about tragedy that strikes so many? It is hard to marry that up when there is so much misfortune and hardship all over the place."*

What came next was a combination of intuitive download and light show that made one hundred percent sense at the time. My wholeness felt its truth and its wisdom. I hope to pass at least some of this to you now.

Imagine a beautiful sphere of rainbow colours, The deep red on the outside merging into orange, into yellow, into green, into blue, into indigo, then violet. In the middle there is the brightest, pure, brilliant white light. Each colour containing different shades and depths of colour, and it is hard to even notice where one begins, and one ends. Even the violet into the white becomes a natural progression.

This is us, the whole of us. Every Soul, every incarnation, every experience of life. All part of the same sphere of energy. All stemming from this beautiful brilliant white light in the centre.

As we incarnate, a droplet of us gets thrown out into this sphere and lands in the perfect place; the perfect setting for us each to settle and grow. The droplet can feel quite separate from the rest, but each droplet has been drawn from the same well in the centre of this sphere. As we settle into this space, this becomes our environment. Everything around us seems to be tinted with the same colour although, as we look around, we see glimpses of the others, the next step or next level, or the ones we may have recognised in the past. As we forget who we truly are and where we truly come from, this scene becomes our reality. As we grow, we take in more and more of the colour around us, feeding that experience, making us become even more grounded in this colour we live in; A self-fulfilling prophecy.

Yet sometimes we have had a fill of that colour, or curiosity gets the better of us. We may even have another experience that may have come from another space within that spectrum and adds a little of their hue into ours. We then notice that maybe life doesn't always have to be red- maybe it can be a little yellow too? Of course, many around you might think you are crazy, because around here everything is red! And how could life be different? If you only open your eyes to see! Yet the yellow feels good to us. It brings in more experience and allows us to perceive things differently, if we allow it to merge with us. If we allow more of the yellow to seep in, then we naturally move into the next stage of orange.

Our purpose is not to jump from one to another to another, as one may be led to believe. Our Soul's purpose is to immerse ourselves and experience all of the colours of the whole spectrum. To absorb enough of the wisdom, the guidance and experience within the red so that you know it to be, and then to know well enough, be curious enough, and ask the questions to be open to the possibility that there may well be other experiences out there.

It is the experience of them all. The light, the dark, the red, the blue, the bright, the dingy, the luminescent and the dense. The whole scale of light and dark and all in-between that we truly know the way of the human; the way of the Soul experiencing life as a human.

We can't skip it. We can't turn away from the yellow because we do not like how things sound like over there or go straight to the violet because things are more comfortable. It is the experience of being seeped into each of the energetic rivers that then builds us to become the light. To return to the brilliant bright light that we emerged from in the centre of this sphere.

You see, white is not the absence of colour. White comprises of all hues of the visible light spectrum. We return back to the essence of all life by experiencing all life.

For many of us, this takes lifetimes, centuries, even millennia. For some, it feels as if we have done the whole sweep in a week. Life isn't a punishment. You don't get 'sent' to a particular colour to suffer. You go to learn and to experience, perhaps even to bring a drop of another hue of the colour wheel into the space that you reside. Perhaps to give others a taste of what may be available.

We are all returning home. We are all doing the very best we can, swimming in our own little pools. This one isn't bad or evil, whilst this one isn't better or lighter. We just all are. Swimming together. Finding our way over rivers, lakes, rapids and seas of colour, to return to the very well in which we all descended from.

We are where we are, but the rest is always around. And perhaps when we pass, or when we find ourselves in sacred holdings, we find ourselves saying,

"Yes, this time I must experience this in order to bring that colour onto my tally, for without it, how can I ever experience white?"

We are asked to judge. We are led to think that this person, or this community, or this type are bad or wrong. That 'we' would never do anything like 'that', because we are too… (insert your righteousness here). But the truth is, we all hold all the capabilities of everything. We all are from the same place, and we all are part of the same sea of life.

When we know that, not only '*could*' we have done something, but that we probably did at some point in our lives; not because we are wrong, bad or evil, but because that was the environment, the surroundings, and the fuel that we ran on; then something happens. Something like compassion or understanding. Something like allowing those other colours that perhaps you have long since grown from to be reignited within you. To allow the light to sift through that once again, so that we are one step closer to home.

These colours can be interpreted as frequency, vibration, circumstances, beliefs, whole era's, jobs, roles, or the emotional scale. It is when we allow it to be, accept ourselves for what we are, and let the light shine through, that the quality of the colour changes. Perhaps then, like the video games I used to play, another star lights up in my repertoire.

We seek to know and then we seek to raise. Through love, compassion, and understanding. Through acceptance of all other experience. Through hope that there is more. Through allowance of all that we were. We shine the light of source within and through it.

Know thyself…

That, dear reader, is the purpose of life.

The Angel Guy

You would think, wouldn't you, that understanding the purpose of life changes everything? I guess it did and it didn't. Sure, in contemplation, meditation, and in group discussions, it was a fascinating idea to ruminate on. However, in the practicalities of the day to day, it is hard not to get caught up in the what's, when's and how's of the situation sat there right in front of you.

I mean, after the fact, when you are reeling that yet another person has let you down or your kids have once again tipped the house upside down, it may be hard to remember the purpose of life in its entirety. (*Don't ever remind me of the incident when the kids, during my first half term with a school aged child, very pregnant and hardly able to move, decided to recruit his 2 year old brother and empty the entire contents of a recently sorted out clothes dresser all over the floor- I cried, a lot*). The idea that this experience is just there to help me earn my orange-coloured badge isn't all that helpful when all you want to do is jump straight into the bright white light. Life can be hard. And no one said it would be easy.

So, I carried on. Still searching, still learning, still wondering where it was leading. I wondered where to turn, and I asked myself who inspired me the most. It was Kyle Gray, the Angel guy, who popped into my head. Here in my mind, there was this young, approachable guy, living his purpose, helping others, shining his light, and I thought to myself,

"*I wonder what he would say to me?*"

No joke, 4 hours later he puts an announcement on the Angel Team page. He has opened his books for a handful of readings, and I knew one had to be mine. So, I put a call out on my social media;

"I need four readings booked today and, if I get them, I am booking a reading in with Kyle Gray."

Within half an hour, I had four people jump right in. I knew that something would come of this, especially when I was so lucky to get one of the remaining slots.

I tell you; I was nervous when I connected with him on Skype. I had arranged for the family to all go out, so for the first time in ages, the house was quiet. He said, *"Hey!"* with his cheeky grin, and then went on to casually change my life!

Kyle went straight into my Angelic team, telling me what a wonderful job I was doing in building up my repertoire. He told me that I am meant to be teaching people and holding space for others. He shared that one of my guides- Sanat Kumara- was standing by me, and he was encouraging me to be seen even more. That my light could go on to support others, but right now I was standing under a wing.

We discussed my mediumship and confirmed what I knew all along: mediumship was not for me. My energy went so much higher and naturally wanted to connect with the guides and the Angels. Once I stood fully into that and stopped trying to dampen this connection down, things would really take off. He was right. I had been sitting in circle for so long, it had become my safe space, but it wasn't my passion. Mediumship as I was practicing, bringing through evidence of life after life, was great training. It was where Kyle himself had first started, but it was too heavy energy for me. He also said I should be teaching it by now.

There was a lot we covered in that hour. He got me. He encouraged me. He made me feel on top of the world. To be honest. I remember thinking,

"Wow! If I can help people feel like this- motivated, encouraged, and hopeful after a reading with me, then I can be safe in the knowledge that I have made a positive impact in others' lives" .

It inspired me to do better. We weren't focused on evidence (although there was much); we were focused upon guidance, practicalities and moving forward. This made way more sense to me than rehashing the past.

Something expanded in me right towards the end of the reading, and washed over me. I had a vision of Kyle and I standing on stage together. I didn't know what it meant, and I couldn't see how we had got there, but the image was so definite. Knees knocking together I said;

"Kyle, I'm not being weird, but I have got to tell you something… I think one day we will be on stage together!" .
(I almost died inside when I actually said it). He smiled that cheeky smile.
"Yes, maybe. You never know Melissa, maybe you'll write a book one day." I shrugged, *"Maybe",* I said. *"I don't know when, and I don't know how, but this is what I see."*

Now I could leave you in suspense here. Because there is a whole heap of journey that happened between that moment and this next one, but that wouldn't be fair, and it is just too exciting to not bring it in right here.

Yet, here is a little side note; something from deep within or far beyond inspired me in that moment. I knew I was in safe hands with Kyle, and I continued to invest in his other courses. Certified Angel Guide was an obvious choice, and the Advanced Angel Card Mastery, Certified Crystal Guide, and his Know your Angels and Know Your Masters courses were all under my belt. Kyle then offered to feature us on his website, and I was one of the first to be listed as one of his certified practitioners. I used my knowledge and love of all I had learned to help support the new members (and old) of the ever-growing Angel Team, plus I had the privilege of meeting Kyle at some of his live events.

Around two years later, Kyle announces that he is going to be running Certified Angel Guide as a live event in London. He asked if any of his certified practitioners be up for helping out.

"Me, me, me!", I pleaded in my head. *"This would be the most amazing thing! Please be me, please be me."*

Like possibly hundreds of others, we put our names forward and a week later I got the email I had been waiting for.

Melissa, we would love to invite you to assist Kyle at his flagship event in London.

Oh. My. Goodness!

I knew this would be big. What an honour! Little old me just doing my thing has this huge opportunity holding the biggest space ever. I would be happy to just be in the room. Not going to lie, I was having a bit (a lot), of a fan girl moment.

Hair done; outfit picked; I was on my way to London Town. It wasn't even just about supporting Kyle; it was also about meeting in person so many of the wonderful people I had met via

Angel Team over the years; many of whom were joining. Plus, the rest of the Angels that were also assisting.

Now we helped set up and the work began. Seeing the room all laid out with these huge round tables, swag bags on every chair, and setting the space energetically you could feel the buzz starting to build. Kyle arrived and it was humbling really to see him prep himself up; you see it doesn't matter how accustomed you are to holding big groups- we all feel 'it'.

The room started to fill, and I was buzzing like I had never buzzed before. Helping people to settle, introducing people, and seeing some familiar faces, before taking a seat in our designated spots at the side of the room.

Kyle opened the space, then pointed over to us.

"I would like to introduce you to my team", he said. *"These are people who have been through my program, and I know and trust them. Girls, I would like to invite you on stage."*

Now you can imagine, as I stood up, I had this moment that was kind of like a Deja-vu, or if you have ever had a premonition that has come true or experienced something that you had dreamt of. I don't really know, but it was like 5 timelines had all come together and led to this moment. The room disappeared as I walked up to the stage, and there I was, s*tanding on stage with Kyle Gray.*

When we introduced ourselves, I couldn't help myself;

"Kyle, do you remember 2 years ago when I said to you that one day, we will be on stage together? Well, EEEK, maybe I am psychic after all!" I had done it; a dream come true."

I remember trying to explain this to my friends who didn't know about Kyle or the Angels that it was like being asked to spar with your favourite sports personality, a guy top of his game, deep in his own connection and following his passion, who wanted to hang out with and trust me! When you are in that kind of energy and you see how many people are lifted up, it's a beautiful thing. Many were having their first real experience of touching the Divine. And wow, did I work my little butt off that weekend! I don't think I left the floor, but it didn't feel like work so much. It felt right. It felt exciting. It felt inspiring. It felt natural. It felt like me, stepping up.

A little over 2 years later, another accolade came when Kyle invited me to become one of his Mentor Teachers for Angel Team. A space that I had spiritually grown up in, a space that helped me grow and know, and now he was inviting me to teach and hold space in my own slot to over 2000 of his paying members. Kyle demonstrated that he trusted me, he handed over his space to me for two evenings and let me shine whilst supporting this group of spiritual seekers.

I know that there are times when experiences change you, and this was one of them. There was something about holding that space for so many people. Being in the presence of the Angels, where I declared,

"I am willing and ready to do this work". It was as if the imposter syndrome that had been stalking me for some time witnessed all of this and said,

"Yep, maybe you have got it after all", which allowed more space in my energy body to hold more space for myself and others.

I had been forever opened up, and this was the start of something special.

The Spiritual Hangover

For 3 days I was on a high, grinning from ear to ear and back again. Telling everyone about my experience, shining on my socials and responding to all the messages and comments from all the people I had met over the weekend.

And then, BAM! One grey morning I hit a wall. It was like a hangover. You know the feeling, a little melancholy, a look around at the mundane of the usual routine and wondering if anything really did change or if you just got swept up in the moment.

It was a real thud, and I remember wanting to climb into bed, turn it all off and just say, *"Not today, thank you"*. My brain wanted to tell me that I was undoing all the development that had happened over the weekend. My imposter syndrome stuck her head back in the mix, waving with a cheery hello after 3 espresso's and asking if anyone wanted a lift to another party. Thing is, this has happened before. In fact, it happened after my Reiki Training, it happened after the Munay Ki, it even happened sometimes after a really great massage. So, whilst lying there with the curtains closed, trying to enjoy the 2 hours I actually had without any children in the house, I took some time. I read a little of the book I had on my shelf, I played a little healing music, I treated myself kindly, I allowed the peace to be around me.

That helped for sure. Slowly my body finding its own recalibration. The out breath to the huge in breath that had happened the weekend before. A reset if you like. A regulation.

Since then, I actually make time following a deep transformational weekend, or if I am holding ceremony. I clear out some time in my diary for something easy, something enjoyable. Maybe a walk in the park with a friend, a massage, or just some time with a book. An early night and some cacao often helps, and oh, I love a long hot soak in a bubbly salt bath following days like these.

This, my friends, is what is known as a Spiritual Hangover. I mean, it makes sense. Being immersed in an energy that upgrades you, that changes you. Being flooded with light that connects to your very cells. Being given information that has wowed you and let you to contemplate things that perhaps you didn't think possible before. Growing your luminous energy body, receiving an energy transmission that clears and revives you. All or any of these things do take a toll on the body!

If you think about yourself as a vessel, in these times you are flooded with this wonderful light. As you do so, all the sediment that has been lying at the bottom can get disturbed. When you are being poured with the good stuff, this sediment is floating around and not really getting a chance to stick. You are on a high, in the vibe and all is good. Then, when you get home, things start to settle. But where that sediment was lying is now filled with something else. A new coding if you like. The old stuff just doesn't fit there anymore; it is surplus to requirements. Or it has transmuted so much that it is now finding its' shape no longer fits in its' old home.

This can make its presence known, and it often does, in weird and wonderful ways. It needs time to integrate and to take effect.

You are no longer in the energy of the weekend, the space being held for you, but you are also no longer in the energy that brought in the original conditions too; for you have changed. You are different. You can never go back to what was normal before, and even though it may feel like a drop way further down than what was your original homeostasis, it's not. You are simply preparing for your upgrade. Your physical catching up with your energy which has already taken camp in a higher dimension!

So, treat yourself accordingly. Yes, I have found out the hard way, searching and clambering to get right back 'up there' because quite frankly I was scared of dropping even further and deeper; but it doesn't work like that. I found that when you truly honour yourself, even talking to the parts of you that are now super scared of this new luminous you, that you are creating and reassuring her that indeed we are all ok, things don't seem so hard.

Perhaps you can enjoy that lazy Sunday morning hangover feeling, and relish that this is one hangover that is actually good for you!

Playing With Fire

Courage comes in many forms. So does stupidity I think. And had I have listened to every one else in my families advice, this next experience would never had come. Yet it did, and the implications of it are still felt today.

Turning up in a sacred land in the Bedfordshire countryside, greeted by friendly faces, a little nervousness and a large tent amongst the grounds, we took our seats.

The circle was opened with some drumming and prayers. We all went up to cleanse our field with sacred smudge. The smoke even felt as if it was communing with me, as it blew in a strange manner around my body. We signed our declaration. The nerves kicked in as it flipped between excitement, denial, nervousness and ego reminding me that we can always bolt if it gets too much.

We were working with the energies of the land. We journeyed with the four corners, connecting with the land spirits as overhead we hear the crows circling overhead. They entered my visions and helped to reveal inner wisdom, and release some of the fear I was holding inside. They handed me a red faceted gem. A symbol of strength, purpose. A gift of protection.

We made mesa bundles for the fire. Filled with small items that we had collected or brought with us; filled with intention and healing and love. As I get up to get my paper, something catches my eye. A single red faceted sequin right there on the floor. I looked around, had someone put it there? Was someone doing a craft project I didn't know about?. Apparently no, none of these. A simple, small red gem had seemingly been placed upon my path as an acknowledgement that maybe my thoughts do have an impact into the physical realm... that spirit were indeed watching out for me, and despite my numerous experiences- maybe a wink to ego to go, see hey, this stuff *is* real.

Feeling more settled and a little bewildered, we sat for the next activity. We had lifted our energy, we had called in the support, we had prepared the sacred space; what else could it be.

She took out a quiver of arrows. Not gonna lie, there was a palpable quiver in the room as she invited us on this next quest.

Before I knew it there was an arrow placed carefully in the centre of my throat, and a woman standing in front of me with a shield. I felt the Earth gather up my legs, and it seemed as if an Eagle had taken hold of me. My arms wide, drawing up, the room started chanting;
"*Magick. Magick*"- my chosen mantra as I felt to awaken more of this in my life. Everything went still.

My inner visions begin working on overdrive. Images of times long passed. Feelings of fear that didn't seem to be mine. Persecution energy entering my awareness. Flashes of faceless beings and screams and darkness all moving across my eyes in milliseconds.

This time was different though. This time, I was in control. This time, it was me that placed the arrow, and it would be me that placed the pressure. I summoned the energy from all around me, gathering it all in my throat; I stepped forward, and with all the mustered strength the arrow snapped right down the centre, clean in two.

Exhilaration filled my whole being. Lifetimes had been healed in that moment, I was sure. Bravery and courage had moved into acceptance and understanding. An energy so deep within, transformed into something higher. A strength I didn't know I had, revealed. I was trembling as I took my seat having a whole inner integrative experience, as I supported the others when they took their place on centre stage.

I felt the change in me as the sacred fire was lit. All of us standing around as we filled this fire with our intentions on this warm summer evening. It roared high and hard. It was mesmerising to watch, and perhaps I could have enjoyed the cracklings and the dance of the flames a little more, had that voice in the back of my head not insisted on reminding me every 3 seconds that these little feet will be walking over that fire very soon.

When the time came I had worked myself up for it. We had done all the empowerment work beforehand. I had just snapped an arrow with my throat, so what could walking on fire really do?! Part of me also wondered (hoped) if it was more of a bravery exercise, and that, maybe once we were walking it wasn't really that hot anyway. Spoiler alert, I was wrong.

The feeling standing there ready to walk the few yards over these burning embers is pretty indescribable. The mind, the body, the energy all with their own opinions. The opinions of well meaning family members swimming in my mind. The Animal guardians who had been so present with me over the day holding and supporting. The coolness of the Earth beneath my feet at this point. The drum beating. The crowd chanting; *magick, magick, magick*. I notice my arms rising, drawing the cool energy of the Earth up my legs and around me. And I walked purposefully over the hot coals. It felt like slow motion. There was no going back. Each step an accomplishment, a leap forward towards the unknown, leaving something old behind. The fire energy propelling me forward and the Earth energy calling me home.

As I stepped back on the Earth, everyone clapped. Exhilaration filing my being. I raised my arms in triumph. My feet were burning, but my heart was shining brighter. I had done it. It was amazing! I couldn't believe it. My ego was kind of in the backseat rolling her eyes, but this intensity coursing through me was not going to let any sabotage or doubt or discouragement rain on her parade.

Two more times I walked that fire. The second and third giving me fire-kisses on my feet. Now, that might sound all romantic, but what that actually is, is a nice way of saying that burning embers are stuck to soles of the foot. It definitely hurt, although I was free from suffering, the Earth was soothing. Each walk giving me something more. It had to be three. Three for my freedom. Three for past present and future. Three for mind body and spirit. Three for me, you and us. It had to be three.

The buzz still surrounding us, it was time to go home. Slipping on my shoes was when ego started having a field day! You're going to regret that tomorrow... the blisters on my feet starting to throb. The long drive home rewarding me with a reminder of what was done each time I placed my foot too hard on the brake.

Yet there was significance to the burns. One right on the reflexology spot of my solar plexus, so I drew the energy in. The healing that my body knew it needed. The fire, and the earth, using my breath- landing in my body. I went to sleep that night and told my body that its job tonight is to heal. And that I will awaken refreshed and alert, and well for my day.

The next morning came after a rested nights sleep. The moment of bliss before remembering, when all of a sudden:

'Oh no, what was I thinking yesterday?!?'

Tentatively one foot went down. The other joined it. I stood up.

No pain! No pain! Nothing! I walked, I skipped to the shower! How is this possible. Body! You are truly amazing. I can't believe it- I mean I *can* believe it; thank you, thank you, thank you. Those blisters had turned to just little flat marks, a reminder of the kisses from the night before. And my body spoke to me in that moment.

Perhaps now, Melissa, you'll know, how much it is we love you.

I didn't think when taking part in a fire-walk that the biggest takeaway would be a love for my body. An awe into its healing nature. A new set of tools to remind me that indeed our bodies are always seeking to heal, as long as we give it the conditions in which to do it in. And that the mind, and intention has a huge impact upon that. In fact the very word intention is used in medical terms when healing a wound.

Our body is a marvellous organism. Supporting us. Full of such wisdom and resource. Sending us messages, listening to us, communing and receiving instruction. I have never looked at my body in the same way again. A sting or a burn reminding me that there is a medicine there, and bringing it intentionally into my body so it can trigger its best response, a cold reminding me to rest, a pain encouraging me to listen…

Maybe it was finally time to pay attention to this body of mine, and all it was trying to communicate with me.

Holy Fire

Sometimes things just call you and they make no logical sense whatsoever. I had been feeling good. I had been growing my Reiki Practice teaching consistently and was now running a monthly Reiki share where local practitioners would come and support each other, as well as giving delicious group healing to one another.

Yet, when I heard three references to the Holy Fire, my ears perked up and my body did that little goose bumpy thing it does when it wants to get my attention. I should have known that something was going to come of this when my brain was saying to me,

"Noooo, you don't need this! You're fine energetically, you don't know the teacher, and what is this Holy Fire thing anyway?"

But the goosebumps persisted, and so did the references. When I looked online, my brain was picking out the reasons why this definitely wasn't the thing for me. Talking about Holy, The Christ Consciousness and being this 'new form' of Reiki, when I considered Reiki as it was, to be a perfect system.

Yet, I found myself somehow on the course, and it happened to just be me and my lovely teacher. I brought with me one of my safety nets, *The Keepers of the Light* card deck by Kyle Gray. Now, I must admit that this deck and I had a funny relationship. At first, I just didn't get it. It had 44 faces depicting different Ascended Masters, which at the time I knew very little about. I would always pull the same card- Dijwal Khul: Dharma

Unfolding. And it didn't really make much sense to me. I even gave the deck away once, but because of my studies with Kyle, I ended up with another copy not long later.

Something however seemed to connect this deck with the Holy Fire. When I asked about 15 times whether the Holy Fire would benefit me, I kept pulling the same card again and again- Rhada: Soul Flame. A beautiful compassionate Goddess, looking kindly at me with knowing eyes, opulently covered in silks and jewels with the words; Rediscover a lost part of yourself. It was all there; Flame, Holy Fire, Rediscovery… plus, it was a few days off of mum duties, and my youngest son was nearly one. So, there I was, waiting to receive no less than 6 energy placements and ignitions, plus the healing journeys.

I don't think I could have anticipated what happened, despite being told what might happen! During the journeys, I met Dragons, Unicorns and Mermaids. I turned into a grain of sand and into vast seas of water. I burned to the ground, and I rose up again, landing on a star. I met my spirit team again and said goodbye to the ones that no longer aligned to me; that was emotional! One in particular I wanted to hold onto for dear life. Whilst she told me she would never abandon me, she also explained that I no longer needed her wisdom to move on. And then, as I moved up to a new level of 'cloud' (how else to describe this scene comprised of floors of cloud in which I could go and replenish and retreat?), I saw a guy. He had a beard and a warm manner. So friendly, so full of love, and so… so light. He took my hand and said nothing. I felt something fill me up, and I am sure my mouth then smiled. He then took me to a lazy river where I lay resting with another who shared with me profound healing and wisdom through words that I couldn't hear but I could understand.

As I drew a card when I returned from this placement, the Jesus card from the deck appeared. For the first time in my life, I opened up to it. I hadn't realised quite the block I had had towards this card and this energy in particular, along with so many of the other energies in the deck. I had recoiled at thinking that I could ever or even ever want to work with any 'religious' figures, let alone Jesus. Brought up Jewish in a Jewish school, he was not part of my past. I was reminded how even in the kids Christingle Services at school I would avoid singing the name of Jesus! I was so unaware of my religious trauma that I held. And now, here, his face shining back at me, I felt a glimpse of the love that this energy can bring.

I moved through the deck, seeing these faces with new eyes. I could feel them, and I could know them. They could know me too. They looked different- warmer. I could hear them! A relationship forming. These cards quickly became my favourite deck, as if I had a posse of 44 wise ones to assist me through every reading, and bring their perspective into the mix. I found myself singing along to *Away in A Manger*. I even found myself on a few subsequent occasions happily speaking with Jehovah's Witnesses and feeling free and open with who I was.

They often say you don't know until you know. And I did not realise this was something I held. I believed myself to be tolerant, accepting and open. I realised this wasn't quite as true as I had thought. It felt as though the Holy Fire was perhaps allowing me to release the guards that I had placed up to protect me against the pitfalls of religion, and the declaration I had made as a teen that I renounced the whole idea of religion. My guides were now stepping up to help me with this. Perhaps through the experiences I had, or perhaps through the World Peace Grid that formed out of the Holy Fire, uniting all the religions of the world to come in peace had affected me. This is what was meant by Holy- Whole, Un-fractured. And now, I had let more light in.

The Holy Fire really did feel to me like an evolution of Reiki. I could feel it working in the background when old patterns were starting to arise. I felt protected by this ring of light around me that I seemed to be connected to. What I could only describe as the Source of Source. It came through in my readings too, connecting with this higher aspect of them that flooded them as the messages came through. I think the energy was starting to form through my voice like a channel. The energy felt good, supportive, and ascending. My ego, however, was trying to scream the house down.

The Ego

The Ego is an interesting thing, right? I had read a tonne of material and listened to many books, particularly of one of my favourite authors, Wayne Dyer, who often described the Ego as Edging God Out. There was speak of killing the ego, transcending the ego, separating from the ego, quieting the ego. Now do not get me wrong, I could listen to Wayne et al all day long, and his teachings about quieting the ego, stopping it being in charge was oh so very helpful, but *something* didn't sit quite right with me about trying to kill this part of myself that seemed to be in the driving seat for so long. I have got to admit, the brain agreed and was very relieved!

The brain really didn't like the idea of edging out of, transcending or separating at all from the very part of me that has actually (what it thinks anyway), kept me safe for so long. I mean, the ego has a job, right? It tells me that I am me, that I like these things, and that I need to do certain things to get here or there. To help me know about consequences. It helps me to achieve, and to take action. Its literal job is to keep us safe from danger. Tracking what we should be scared of. Talking us down so we don't put our head above the parapet. Stopping us being ejected from the tribe. Helping us to fit in, and to act in certain ways in certain environments. It certainly has its uses. Sure, if we are spending our lives saying, *"Om"* at the top of the mountain, it may be surplus to requirements. However, right here, in the English countryside, as a mum, wife, friend, business owner and the countless other roles I am trying to successfully hold down, I am pretty sure it has its uses.

So, I wondered, what if it is not about killing the ego, or even transcending it? How can we get this thing in check so that it goes along with what I want? How can I trust it more, so it doesn't throw a hissy fit every time I try and do something that is going to better my spirit?

Turns out healing is the way. Healing the ego! Healing! What is healing? Bringing light, becoming healthy, restoring its vitality, making whole. Got to be honest, my ego was a little unsure, but it seemed happier with that than the other options that were laid upon the table. But who knew that when you set about to heal the ego that it likes to shout and scream really loud just to make sure that you're listening, especially when you aren't?!

The Ego, it turns out, doesn't really have a mind of its own. It is just running on what it seems to be right. Things we asked it for help with as a toddler when we had almost zero power over our lives- safety, identity, feeling special when we didn't, helping ourselves be heard, or stopping ourselves being a target. It does what it is told for the pure aim of its (and your) survival. It is the part of us after all that won't survive after we part this Earth, so it is just doing its very best to keep you safe. It runs on the programs you feed it, and those that are being fed from the collective. But it doesn't have its own fuel source.

So, I wondered, what might happen if I sourced it with safety? If every time it piped up, I said,
"Ok, let me hear what you have to say."
Like these little chestnuts:
Ego: *"I am not good enough for that."*
Me: *"Ok, that is an interesting opinion. Thank you for reminding me how much I want to do well at this."*
Ego: *"I can never pull that off."*
Me: *"Thank you for helping me understand where I need to do more work."*

Ego: "They'll all laugh at me if I do that."
Me: "Interesting you think that, maybe I can add some humour to my work."

So, it went on. And wow, did she pipe up! The more I stepped up, the more in fact she piped up. But the more I listened, the more she shrugged with a, *"Well, I tried to warn you"* kind of attitude. And then I would send her off to do her job.

"Hey", I would say, *"can you give me something useful to work with please? Can you help me find something that will help me feel safer, more prepared, more trustworthy, more confident, more competent… Let's do this. Together."* Out breath.

It was as if she was my overzealous risk assessor, yet now she was satisfied that we had the check list, and nothing bad was going to happen. So then when I gave her the pay cheque at the end of the month, it fuelled her to know she was safe and sustained.

She stopped seeing all *'others'* as the enemy. She helped me find solutions to the problems she was bringing up too. We could dialogue between her and a higher, more conscious part of me. She no longer needed to run the show, and all this evidence I was piling onto her, let her understand that it was OK, no one was coming for us this time.

Of course, it is a work in progress. I would love to say, yep, ego healed and check this out, but that would, well, be ego talking. It is a process. And she is a part of me that I honour, yet no longer obey. The work comes in truly knowing which voice is which because she will take reign if we give her free rein, so we continue, bringing healing, making safe, and becoming healthy.

All until it brought something rather large to my attention.

The Elephant In The Room

That was how I felt. *The Elephant.*

I was looking through the pictures of the weekend at the Angel Guide training. This was one of the proudest moments of my life but, as I looked at the photos of me, I felt ugly. I felt huge. I felt like everyone would see that I was not full of light; I was full of cake.

You see, with all of the energy work I had been doing, and the holding of space for others, plus the toll of 3 pregnancies in 5 years, my body had been crying for some attention. I was so ungrounded, and my body was craving for it. So, it turned to where it knew it could get some sustenance and earth energy. Food.

My relationship with food and my body hadn't, like many young girls, been the healthiest. Growing up in the 80s and 90's it was all body image. I had heard my family, my friends and all the pretty girls on TV talking about weight, and I was even a teen subscriber of all those toxic magazines which no young mind should be allowed.

I had spent the last few years firstly nourishing my mind. I wanted to learn everything and anything about all the techniques, processes, philosophies and theories, and had saturated myself in that. I had then moved on to the Soul, bringing things into practice, taking all the energy medicines and feeling the feels. Channelling healing and holding space. Sitting with crystals and feeding my energy.

All the while of me saying more, more, more, my body was responding by holding more, more, more. More water, more food, and wanting more sugar and carbs to sustain it all.

I could see my body was changing, but I rarely looked at myself in the mirror (isn't that ego?), and I was usually the one behind the camera taking pictures of my kids. So, I did what was easiest for me to do, and completely ignored what I looked like and felt like in my body. I told myself I was happy and beautiful, and people shouldn't judge people on their weight, to quit fat shaming and that people are so much more than their body. (true). I told myself I had transcended this body and it wasn't about this meat suit that I wore.

But when I was faced with the reality that I was about to full on discard a bunch of pictures of me literally realising a dream came true, it hit me full throttle in the eye.

I hadn't transcended anything. I had turned away from myself. This body that was my very vessel that kept me here. This beautiful body that I had essentially ignored and abused because I was too busy seeking enlightenment. This body that held me through this and was reaching out for heavy foods to try and bring some balance into my life.

This body that I had stuffed right back into this bag of *'let's deal with this another time... like, never'* was there looking at me in the face. I saw myself hating on myself, and it tore me apart. How could I feel this way about myself? I knew I was a being of Love. I was a steward of this Earth, and I couldn't even steward myself. Isn't my physical body my personal Earth plane? I wanted to blame everything but me. I even went to the doctor who declared me obese and prescribed me 12 weeks at one of these weight loss clinics. My body screamed at me *NO!* I had to work it out for myself. Was this ego protecting me, or a true intuition that this isn't the right path?

I was down on myself. Christmas was coming and I couldn't trust myself anymore. I knew that things had to change. So, I did what I do. I bought a crystal (apatite- apparently it helps), I sat with my energy medicines and allowed them to flow through me.

I asked into the void,

"What do I need to do to bring me back to the vibrant Earth Mama that I am?"

Growing A New Body

Browsing through my audiobook collection to prepare for a number of long car journeys I had coming up. I had quite a collection sitting on my various accounts, and one stood out. It was called *'How to Grow a New Body'* and was written by Alberto Villoldo. This was a man I was familiar with because of his development of the Munay Ki. I didn't even check what it was about, but it gave me the feels, so I got in the car and off I went.

Now, I am listening to this book, which is talking about how we eat, and how it affects our body, our DNA, and our energy. He speaks of eating like our Ancestors. My brain was saying to me,

"NO, NO, NO! You could NEVER do that. Impossible! No Bread? No Cake? No Chocolate? This sounds like torture!"

My body however was giving me a completely different set of information. My fingers kept pressing next chapter, and I continued to return to this book journey after journey. When a friend then came round and told me of how she had been doing Keto and loved it, and then my son's 6-year-old friend was also on the same diet to manage epilepsy, I figured there was someone trying to tell me something. I didn't do much about it at first, until one morning a couple of weeks later.

I was feeling a little bit lousy. I wasn't all that hungry, for once. Suddenly I heard myself announcing to my husband,

"I am starting this Keto thing. No bread, no pasta, no potatoes: no carbs." I don't think he believed me, but my plan was to keep this up for five weeks until I went on holiday.

Within a few days, my body was thanking me already. I had some of the symptoms you can get when you starve your body of glucose, but I was already feeling less bloated and a lot cleaner. I figured now would be a great time to try my first experience of Kambo. Now, if you are of the faint of heart then please, skip ahead a couple of paragraphs! But this medicine had been calling me, and something told me now was the right time.

I turned up at the Shaman's space, where she had set up the altar. We cleaned my energy and discussed my intentions. Kambo is a frog medicine which comes from the Amazon rainforests. It is essentially a frog poison, which, when combined with an intention and a secure sacred space, allows you to purge both physically and energetically what you are holding in your body. Over the 4 times I had sat with Kambo, I held various intentions from releasing anger, to releasing fear, to cleansing my body, to the last one of purging all of my identities (*I got brave*).

I must say, the first time wasn't the most pleasant of experiences. I, you see, love to be in control. I do not like to be at the mercy of anything, and my dignity is something I hold very dear! So, when the medicine entered my body, my natural reaction was to hold on! Luckily(!) for me, the Shaman held me through it, coaxing me out. Eventually, the release was so freeing and expansive that I let go. I let go of the bitterness I had held. I let go of the anger towards the past, the people that let me down, the way I had treated others and myself. The things I had done to my body, and the way I had spoken to it. On my final Kambo- almost 2 years after the original sitting- I let go of everything I knew myself as. Every identity that had been placed upon me and I asked for only my true essence to remain.

Each session was different, and each session left me changed. Each session of being with this powerful, humbling and cleansing medicine helped me to release more of the binds and step more into this version of me that I was becoming.

The first time I left there skipping. I felt so clean and clear. I was a channel of pure divinity. I wanted no more poison or density to be in my body ever again! This was the start of an 18kg weight loss- a quarter of my body weight shed as I released the shackles of programming, greed, mild depression and of some self-sabotage I had found myself in. My food became something that I enjoyed, was satiated but no longer controlled my life. I discovered intermittent fasting and eating one healthy, vibrant meal a day. I discovered the assertiveness to request my meal without the carbs when dining out rather than the *"Yes, I'll have it as it comes."* I discovered a willpower that I didn't even know I had, and a relationship in my body that felt like we were a team rather than in battle about how any food enjoyment was going to leave me lethargic, guilty or hating myself.

I don't attribute this all to the Keto way of eating. I attribute this to listening to what my body needed, to being in the right place, the right frame of mind, and discovering the right thing for me at the time. It acted as a reset for my relationship with my body and with my fuel source. Nine months in, I started a yoga practice, which became my sanity. Watching how my body could move, from the first day in Yoga class when I could barely manage a Downward Dog, mismatching my breathing, and toppling at the first sign of taking even one limb off the floor, to starting to feel better. To being able to comfortably reach my toes. To my first Chaturanga where I finally didn't collapse in a heap, and the Pigeon where I didn't want to cry.

My body evolved, and so did my relationship with it. As I shrunk physically, my energy body could grow, and I was finally ready to take up more space instead of trying to shrink away.
I realised how grateful I am for this beautiful body and how, if I truly want to be an Earth Keeper of this world, I need to keep this Earthly vessel nourished and evolved.

After all, it always starts with us.

Failing To Prepare

An old boss had often told me, *"Fail to Prepare, Prepare to Fail."* His words would often ring in my ears before I was running a workshop or sitting in a session. However, preparing for a reading or a healing isn't very easy. I mean, of course, you can be clean, and be physically nourished and watered etc. You can have your paraphernalia going on. You can know your cards like the back of your hand, but you never knew what is about to happen. So, short of the intention that I held before every sitting;

'Thank you Angels, Guides and my Highest Self for bringing through messages of love and hope. May they be received in a way that is loud and clear and understandable and leave us both feeling better than before we began. Thank you for keeping my ego out of the way and bringing through messages only of divine love' (make up your own to make it yours), there wasn't much else I could do.

For my workshops, which were now becoming more and more regular, things were different. I had partnered up with my magical friend Golden Paw Grant, running monthly meditation moon circles. My job was to channel the meditations and his job was to lead the sound healing. Grant was the very man who had birthed my beautiful Shamanic drum, and between us we had quite a range of singing bowls and sound healing instruments. These workshops started with 4 or 5 of mainly our friends turning up. They soon went to 15 or more. Each month I would check out what was happening in the skies, and the particular energies of the moon. I would write out a theme of the meditation and be prepared for the little pre-talk I would do, and a rough idea of where the meditation was going to go. I turned up ready, allowing room for inspiration to come in during the meditation.

One particular day- which happened to be the same as the first Kambo day- I had zero time for prep. I was in that giddy space that feeling so clean and connected can leave you; in a kind of Que Sara Sara (whatever will be will be) way. So, I turned up for this first meditation of the new year with no idea of what was going to happen, with a bag full of crystals and a card deck.

To my surprise, there was around 25 people in the room. Word had gotten around about Grant and my healing sessions and the magic they created. Words like *cosmic, heavenly*, and *deep* would be used, so people turned up expecting something.

I was a little petrified! There were brand new people that I had never seen before. People brought their friends along and there was a buzz of excitement. I had zero clue what I was going to say, where we were going to go and what on Earth (or elsewhere) was going to happen. *Prepare to fail, fail to prepare*, I heard inside my head. And then I heard another voice. A whisper, but this whisper felt a lot more convincing as it brought goosebumps around my body.

'*Trust us, we have got this*'. Okay…

I welcomed everyone. I wasn't sure if anyone picked up on my nerves, nor if they could see that my face felt like it was on fire. Good job the lights were dim, and we were sitting by candlelight. 3 cards were pulled which I explained would set the energy of the night. My old friend Djwhal Khul appeared. I am sure more as a wink to me- trust in the path- and I invited everyone to close their eyes.

As soon as I began to speak, an energy began to course through my body. It seemed to rise up from the Earth, as Grant gently beat the drum. My voice began to change ever so slightly as the images in my head appeared faster and faster. A journey was unfolding right in front of my eyes. I was there with them. Grant, forever in sync, was picking up on my subtle cues as we journeyed through the cosmos, being touched by Angels, and being greeted by a deeply healing energy. And then, as the drumbeat got deeper and the words ran out, I felt something else come over me. I could hear in my head the symbols I had learned during my Karuna Reiki training. Symbols that were most powerful when they were sung.

I could not sing in front of all of these strangers! No one had signed up to that; until I did. My voice opened and not even I recognised the sound that came out. Deep yet soft chants of these ancient symbols gently drifted out of me. The energy in the room changed, and the quietest stillness swept across the room. We were entranced.

I held that space with a team of other beings and had never felt more supported in my whole life. I hadn't failed to prepare anything. In fact, in many ways, this whole thing had been pre-arranged. I understood now. Yes, prepare, but prepare in energetics, prepare in intent, prepare in the structure, and then surrender to the joys and the beauty of the possibilities that are available to us when we allow for divine inspiration to land.

I wasn't preparing to fail. I was preparing to be caught, time and time and time again.

Who Are We Surrendering To Anyway?

Surrender it.
urrender it.
urrender it?

I was never entirely sure what that meant. I mean, who or what is it exactly I am surrendering to? Am I surrendering to some divine plan that had been placed before me, that I am simply acting out the role for? Has the Universe got great ideas for me? And, if so, who decided that in the first place?

And how much of my life do I actually need to surrender? And how does that fit in with intention? To be honest, surrendering my whole life out just doesn't feel right. Surely, I have more say in my destiny than someone else, or is that just ego talking?

Yet one day I was contemplating this. One day, after placing on my platinum shield and stating:

'*My declaration of intention is to serve my source, I commit to serving my highest power, wholly, fully and completely*' I realised something- if we are simply surrendering, we could be surrendering to anyone, or any thing. Yet if I am committed to serving my highest source, then what it is I am surrendering to has another agenda all together.

You see, it is *possible* that not everything out there has our best interests at heart. Perhaps there are influences that like to manipulate, discourage, or help us to feel less powerful. And I am not necessarily talking about malevolent forces here, but we notice this with our media, advertising agencies, governing bodies even. Agencies that I certainly wouldn't want to surrender any of my will to!

It is vital that we take ownership of ourselves, our lives and our destinies. I do not believe that the Universe has a grand plan for us. I believe that the Universe is responding to our needs, wants, and desires- our very vibration. Should we allow ourselves to simply be pulled into the most dominant direction, it may not be what we truly want or desire, but it may well bring us to that which we *believe* we want, need or desire. Note to self, these two things aren't always the same.

Surrendering, if not done properly, can leave us powerless. It can leave us manipulated into carrying on doing what we have always done, or worse, drawing us down rabbit holes that certainly do not serve us in reclaiming our power.

My thoughts are that this journey that we find ourselves on is so much bigger than that. So much more empowered than that. For we are here to discover who we are, to understand how we find satisfaction, joy, compassion and love, as well as to figure out how we serve others. To learn, to grow, to heal. To acquire knowledge and experience and turn that into wisdom. To ascend and become more into our God-self- our true nature- away from the programming and the patterns that we have inherited from the past.

Should I surrender to all of that? Surrender to my shortcomings, surrender to my unhealthy habits, surrender to the way that society currently is? Let all that be in charge? Not on my watch.

So then, what is all this talk about surrendering about?

AHA! Intention. Intention is key. Intention informs our actions. Our actions inform our vibration. Our vibration informs the Universe. Why would we do all these practices to raise our vibration, to know ourselves, to connect in with our highest self? They help us to consciously seek to improve. To consciously endeavour to find enlightenment. To know ourselves. And who or what is better equipped at guiding that than our Highest Self? This is not our high-*er* self, who may only be one or two or three notches above us in our vibrational alignment, but our high-*est* self. The part of us that is taking all of our experiences, that knows all of our incarnations, that understands the biggest picture and how it all pulls together to create the spectrum that will bring us back fully into the pure brilliant white light. So, we seek to connect there. We declare our intention every day.

I **commit** *to serving my highest power.* **My** *highest power.* **My highest** *power.*

And that is a two-way street.

We make the connection, and we ask for guidance. Not from anywhere apart from the space that has our highest evolution in mind. We ask for guidance that helps us to create our intention. We speak that out to the Universe, who in turn responds… and then we surrender. I surrender in the deep knowing that my very highest aspect of myself is guiding me and knows things a whole lot better than I do. The signs, the synchronicities, the nudges, the opportunities… now I know it is not just my phone reading my mind and sending me that next product I just *have* to buy. Now I know that I am divinely led by Source, my Source.

And that might just change everything.

The Committee

As I became more sensitive, as I was becoming more involved with holding space for others, bringing messages through and being an open channel, things started to get a little noisy. Now, it was not just the very thoughts in my own head that I had to navigate. Now there was a whole spirit world that potentially had access to me, and me to it.

It can be pretty tempting to be open for business, so to speak. It's beautiful being in divine company, and it can feel so heart-warming, so inspiring, and so awe inspiring to receive these messages and energies. There's always someone or something there to listen to you, and, if you listen back, to offer advice.

However, sometimes it feels as if there's a whole board of indecision in my head. All these different opinions and viewpoints if I ask that fatal question... what *should* I do? Asking *that,* is opening ourselves up to all of it, and there may be one hundred thousand different opinions in the spirit world about what *they* think you should do. It, however, is never about *should*. Only you can decide that... otherwise we are asking this multitude of spirit to take control of our life, and well, that is not their job.

I had always thought really that if we *'put it up to spirit'* that we will get the best possible answer. I hadn't truly considered how much 'spirit' and variety there was.

The Psychic Realm - This is all the energies that are emitting from humans. Our energy fields that surround our being, holding all of the memories and the potentials, the desires, and our manifestation vortexes. When we open out to receive energy, this can often be the first point of call. After all, it is something very familiar. We are used to being person on person. We converse and often feel into what others are experiencing. We entangle ourselves with others all of the time! So, when we open our energy body to *'get the guidance'*, for many of us, this will be the first realm that we discover.

The Collective Unconscious - This field which perhaps is fed by the psychic realm, yet has been around us, holding all of our collective beliefs. I often wonder if this is our default (at least for adults anyway) that informs our invisible world. This can be super useful to dip into, of course, but do we *really* want it informing our highest decisions?

The Spirit World - for the sake of ease, let's define this in this context as the space we go when we pass. The Spirit of Humans that are no longer in body. Our loved ones who live on in our heart. They are never far. And no, it is not as if I feel that Spirits are roaming the Earth, waiting on us on hand and foot- I am pretty sure they have plenty of places to be and see- but I don't think they are ever very far. Now, we know from our own lives that all of our loved ones, friends, family all have an opinion, right? And rarely do they all align with each other, let alone our own. So, I wonder what ever made me think that the 'spirit' world would have all the answers. Well actually they do, and that is the problem… between them they probably have *all* the answers and then some, but they probably aren't entirely the right ones for us! Let us also remember (noted), that it is not just the loved ones we know that make up the spirit world. There are potentially billions of spirits we could have access to… so who exactly are we asking?

The Deities - The divine beings, worshipped by many over different religions and cultures. The Gods and Goddesses, who all have their own roles and agendas. You only need to think of the Ancient Greek culture and look how the different beings got on with each other to wonder whether you would want them all, let alone even two of them, in your head at any one time! Now I love working with the deities, because they mostly have a very specific role. This one rules the sun, this the moon, this one brings abundance, and this one fierce power... they can be helpful if you know what kind of energy you want to tap into. Yet, asking the goddess of destruction to help you with your business making decision... well you get where I am going.

The Angels - The messengers, or in my experience, the expressions of God. Made up of Guardian Angels (there is rarely a reason why you wouldn't call upon yours!), the Angelics and the Archangels; there are so many different expressions. Angels have, for the most part, never incarnated on this Earth, and sit if you like in the higher realms, bringing you different facets of the divine- different personalities or natures of God. They can bring you a very high perspective, and certainly a very high frequency into your situation. Yet, they haven't experienced what it is to be human. Whilst they have such wisdom, empathy and honour for us, sometimes you just want someone who has walked a mile in your shoes to assist.

The Spirit Guides - The realm of guides, who can well cross over with the 'spirit world' as outlined above. I like to think that when I pass over, I will be a Spirit Guide, perhaps even to some of you who are reading these words- if you want me! Each guide has a specialism, an experience, a talent or a gift that can assist and guide you. As they have walked this Earth before, they have been in your shoes, and can offer you counsel based on your needs. I wonder quite how many guides there are in the world. The teacher guides, the helper guides, dream guides, animal guides, ancestor guides, to name but a few. And, just like humans, they come with a whole manner of experiences and intents.

Ascended Masters - Humans who came and fulfilled a mission on Earth, healed their ego and took their place to help guide humanity. Many you may have heard of- like Christ, or Buddha or St Germaine, many may be more obscure to our histories, yet each has experienced something that can help humanity. Like the Angels and guides, these beings are omnipresent and can assist us when we call upon them. They are unique in the sense that they have healed egos and so can seem to resonate like a deity or an Angel, yet they know what it takes to be a human.

Star Ancestors - Our star families. We all come from the stars; our very bodies are made up of these. Pleiadians, Sirian, Lyran, Arcuturian, Andromedan, and Orion. All with different personality traits and wisdom, which ensures they have different missions, directions and opinions.

And then of course, we have the very keepers of the Earth, Gaia and the nature guides and the animal wisdoms. Even the spirits of our animals and plants that we can be in commune with.

No wonder it can get confusing and overwhelming. I was driving myself a little mad at times! Who do I call in? Which one should I work with? Why isn't 'Spirit' giving me a clear answer? The answer was there all along. There are so many variations, so many potentials, so many opinions, and such a vastness of opportunity to connect, that we simply cannot just throw it out there and expect for them all to have the perfect answer.

These teams and these energies are here to support us. They are like a community or a network that we can choose to go and hang out with at certain times or draw upon. It is neither wise nor practical to want them all to come to the same party, in a small room right there in your head. And so, I learned. Connect in with my highest self first. Ask for the guidance on what it is that you want clarity on. Ask for the healing for what it is you need the soothing on, and then either call upon one you know can help, or ask your highest self to lead you to the greatest guide that can serve you on your path. Sure, thank the Angels, Guides, Deities, or the Ancestors to walk with you and assist you, but know that *you* are walking this path, *your path*, and they are not here to do the work for you.

Request help, surrender. Know that these beings are always just a breath away but know that the best voice that is in your head for the majority of the time is your very own... your own true self who witnesses and hears it all.

The silent voice. That is the one that really matters. As we begin to open up, it can feel overwhelming. I know! I have been there. And perhaps this helps explain a little why. There is an abundance of knowledge, wisdom and healing around us... yet it is your light and your inner voice that is always in the front. Make time to listen to her. Bring your power back to you. And surrender to your highest wisdom, for she truly has your back.

Through the good times, and the harder ones, that light is always there.

The Shadow

Spending my time moving towards the light, seeking the light, and immersed in light-filled activities was exactly what I needed. It helped me to create this field of possibilities. To help me know how powerful I am. It helped me to understand that there was magic, healing and light in the world, and I needed that to motivate me, to pull me forward and to help me discover so much.

Yet there were things in me that didn't seem to shift. Behaviours and emotions that felt just so rotten. There were times I was so sure that things had never felt quite so bad before. Was I just numbing to it previously? Did I just not make space for it? If I was ascending and drawing in more light, healing and growing, why did I drop so low?

But that is the point, isn't it? As more light pours in, it reveals the shady areas. The areas that weren't touched. The old dusty cupboards and unopened bags, filled with goodness knows what, suddenly become apparent. I mean, when it is dark, we can't see the shadows, right?

Yet, no one had told me this before. I had only been taught to seek the light and, in doing so, I so often turned my head away from the dark. Letting the shadow fall behind me, out of sight. But out of sight is not out of mind. Not when the shadow was filled with heavy baggage- and I am not talking about the big lump of Lemurian quartz I carried in my bag.

The higher we rise, the further the fall. I realised when I wasn't grounded and where I ignored the signs, that the drop felt so much more uncomfortable than when I was operating on that level in the first place. So, I did the only thing I could do- armed with my torch light, I set to heal those shadows.

What I thought I would be discovering was the source of my anger. What I thought would happen was that I would take all that I was ashamed of, all that no longer fitted with my view of myself, and pick it up and drag it out kicking and screaming by the scruff of its neck. However, as I began to ask myself the deep questions, cradling in my arm all that I rejected, it was a completely different story.

I had thought the point was to kill the ego, that was what I was taught, but what I wanted was to be more comfortable in myself, to not be afraid anymore.

I didn't even know I was afraid in the first place.

This fear was causing me to hide my light in ways I didn't even consider. Putting myself down in front of other spiritual teachers and leaders. Hiding what was on my mind with friends and family because I didn't think they would understand. Stopping myself from doing the things that gave me joy- and when I did do them, downplaying how I felt because I didn't want to be judged.

These things I kept hidden were leading me to judge others. Others that could have been my biggest cheerleaders, or my highest teachers. All because I was recognising in them what I wouldn't or couldn't see in myself. Judging, criticising, fault finding- all the while looking outwards and, in my mind, putting others down, because that is a whole lot easier than lifting myself up.

As this was masking any true satisfaction in many areas of my life, I was storing the energy that would come out in either outbursts of anger and frustration, lead me to the kitchen cupboard for a sugar fix, or fill me with this stored up anxiety that I compressed down for fear of what might unleash if I let it out. The more I faced it, the more I realised that these parts of me- these valid, scared and unsure parts of me- they didn't need to be cut out or rejected. They needed to be faced and seen because, as they did, they were no longer shadows. They were no longer big balls of energy that were stuck in the corner that in inappropriate times would come out like in a trickster game of whack-a-mole. All of this light I had been cultivating was actually shining upon these parts and soothing them, bringing them up, allowing to be seen and accepted.

It was a moment where I saw every single judgement and criticism that I had made of others was nothing to do with them. It wasn't them that made me angry, mad, or disappointed- it was me. It was an unhealed or unseen part of me that was coming up and making me feel so damn uncomfortable so I could finally understand it and seek to help and make it better. Make it whole. Make me whole. These rejected parts of me had become egregious energy that seemed to have taken a life of their own. But no longer, because *now* I was ready to see and to feel.

I learned something else as I explored about this shadow of mine. These parts of me I didn't let the light hit, had gold in them. It wasn't all anger, judgement, greed, lack and fear. It was also confidence, self-assurance, opinions, leadership, authenticity, ease and courage. But, because I had spent so long acting in a way that I had deemed safe and looking outside of myself for the answers- these parts of me were never recognised, so they just waited- patiently- in that dusty cupboard ready to be opened and tried on for size. When I did, they fit like a glove.

My shadow was not my enemy. It wanted to be my friend. It wanted to help me and keep me safe. It wanted to be seen and understood, and I realised now in how many ways it helped me to find it. By bringing discomfort when I wasn't allowing my full expression. By bringing to me people I admired and allowing me to feel the envy that they could just do it, when I wouldn't let myself do the same. By wanting to express when my guard was down, or my energy was low. When it was just too hard to wear the mask of this perfect individual that I had conjured up in my head. I had admired authenticity, yet I had only allowed for others to see this perfect self. The mask needed to be dropped, for it was uncomfortable, heavy and it no longer fit.

So, I dropped it. I told people that I lost my temper. I let others see my doubts. I shared whilst leading sold out retreats that, yes, I got nervous beforehand. I allowed myself to look in the mirror and truly see my body that I had been hiding over ever larger clothes. I told other teachers and mentors how much they meant to me, and how they helped to lighten my load. And, when I got angry, tired, or overwhelmed, I quit blaming everyone else, and just put my hand on my stomach and said, *"Hey, I see you, what do you need?"*

I began to accept compliments. That was a hard one. I was so used to deflecting. *"Who me? What, this old thing? Oh, it was nothing."* They all turned into a simple thank you. Thank you through the tremble and the flushed face but thank you. I accepted the gift.

Through all of that, something magical started to happen. Judgements lessened, and I stopped finding the need to criticise others and blame them for their actions. I was becoming less pushed and pulled by outside circumstances. Compassion for others first of all became easier. An understanding of who they are and what they are doing. When my old friend judgement did come back online, a gentle reminder would come in and ask me,

"What is it in them that you are not seeing in yourself?"

That is a hard lesson to learn at times. All the things! All the things I was so used to blaming others for. All the things I had absolved all responsibility for. All the projection and the victimhood. Even the camaraderie I would feel when hanging out with others who loved a gossip and a moan. None of it was true because none of it was outside of me. And, when I got over that ego response of blame, I realised what it was that was yearning for some help, what in me wished it could be a little more like them, or times when I even did the very thing I was bitching about. Once the ego had settled down and realised that this was indeed a safe practice, it became the most empowering thing I had ever done.

It is all me. It is not about how others are, trying to control how they behave, being disappointed when I was let down or this didn't live up to expectations. It was simply me, and how I behaved, responded, and how I allowed for those emotions to move. This is the spiritual way I discovered, to allow for it all, without judgement, in full wakefulness. Yes, of course, it took a while for this to become a habit. I wish I could say it was all comfortable, but it wasn't. Yet, one thing is for sure- if it wasn't for that understanding and that exploration, I would still be carrying a bag of heavy-duty rocks and dirty socks up this mountain.

Dreaming Myself Awake

Embracing my shadow and integrating these parts of me took some energy for sure. In those periods, my dreams started becoming intense and deeply revealing. The eight hours a night was fast becoming part of my spiritual practice.

When I discovered Lucid Dreaming, things became very interesting. The closest I had got before was my kiss with the Angel of Death some years ago. Now I was having many dreams of flying and reaching high, and I was recording my dreams in a little book beside my bed.

A young Buddhist guy, Charlie Morley, had led me through a Shadow Retreat, holding me through all I had described in the previous chapter, he was also an avid Lucid Dreamer; so it was natural that the topic of discussion would go this way. Lucid Dreaming is a very unique state, in which you are having a sleeping dream, and you realise you are dreaming whilst in the dream.

It so happened at the time that my youngest son was crawling into bed with us in the middle of the night, so I used this nightly opportunity to practice my lucid dreaming state. I would each day, every now and then when something out of the ordinary happened, check if I was dreaming. This would become a habit, and the majority of the time my hand would be its regular shape and size. Yet sometimes, I would look, and my hand would grow an extra finger, or the numbers on the clock would be completely wrong, or I would jump and fall through the floor. In these times, I would know I was dreaming!

And oh, such fun I had! Running off buildings and flying high. Moving through objects and feeling how real they felt against my skin, a true sensation but no pain and no suffering. The flying... The flying was my favourite, and the diving deep and breathing underwater, exploring lands I didn't know.

Walking through a wall must be one of the strangest sensations I have ever known. It is very interesting as I learned more about the self-limits we impose upon ourselves. How very often I would fly, reach the ceiling and try to keep on going, knowing that this roof is merely a projection of my very own imagination. Sometimes the concrete would stretch and mould. Sometimes I would feel it wrapping around me. At times, I would go so high and so far, that it was like that gooey slime the kids would play with. Yet I couldn't break through. Despite knowing it was mine, I would be bounced all the way back down, the force waking me up.

Until one day. I had read all the books, and learned so much from Charlie and other dream practitioners, and by this point clocked up some wonderful experiences in the lucid state. I had just run a workshop on Lucid Dreaming in my local venue and was discussing this. I was sharing my experiences and some of my dreams, willingly allowing some of my inner workings to be shared with the group. I had told them, I have never been able to see what was on the other side of this wall. Just a couple of days later, I found myself lucid in a dream and I began to walk through a wall. It felt like Styrofoam around me, and I could hear the wall as well as feel it. It was so thick! I was fascinated by the experience, and I kept calm and told myself to keep moving slowly forward and I will break through. To my surprise, one more step and my head popped through to see this beautiful cave. Inside was a body of azure water which I stepped into. I allowed my body to become immersed into this warm water, and in my dream, I fell back to sleep as I noticed the hole in the wall that I had come through had sealed itself up again. I had broken through and found a deep soothing healing on the other side. Who knew what this then led to, or if this was a culmination of all the work I had been doing on myself, but this is a dream I will never forget.

When we dream you see, everything in that dream is a projection of self. Speaking a very unique language of symbology and archetypes, as we enter our dreamscape we open up to our whole inner world. All that is repressed over the day, all that our ego does not allow for us to see, all the shadow we turn away from or things we don't give time to have freedom to talk. This language that our subconscious mind knows and responds to deeply. Our body talking to us. Our higher selves communicating through. Our guidance team contemplating with us. Our energetics having the freedom to share all it needs, if only we will listen.

The dreams, however, were not all flying and butterflies. I became very interested in the healing aspects of dreaming. Aware that the power of lucid dreaming can be more influential than meditation, hypnosis, and conscious awakening work, I wanted to use these opportunities to carry on healing. So, one day, as I found myself encountering a strange clock that was dripping numbers in a yellow house that was unfamiliar to me, I noticed I was dreaming.

In kind of a panic (which can happen because of the pure excitement of finding yourself in a state that is not governed by any of the natural laws of Earth), I called out,

"SHOW ME FEAR." Straight away my brain was screaming, *"Melissa, what are you doing?"* Yet I said it again,
"Show me fear!"

To my surprise, this little old man with a bald head started walking down the stairs. My body naturally recoiled, and I started to propel backwards at 100 miles an hour. Yet he just stood there, looking at me. I was intrigued. I was expecting spiders or zombies, or the classic standing naked in front of all your classmates type scenario, but what was in front of me was this harmless looking man.

Using all my might, I pulled myself back until I was standing face to face with him.
 "Hello", I said, and then I took all the courage I could muster and reached out to give him a hug.
"Embrace your fears", Charlie had said, so I literally did. I embraced my fear and hugged it tight.

Some months later I bumped into Charlie- the Lucid Dreamer- at an event and told him of my dream. He laughed at my bravery and informed me that I had probably just saved myself about seven years' worth of psychological counselling! I think he was right. I became braver then, more willing to be seen. Who knows how much that changed my course.

It is amazing really how when you think about dreaming, how real things seem at the time. Even unbelievable scenarios like riding a six-headed donkey or having dinner with the president, we just accept them for how they are and that they are true. It makes me wonder how much in waking life we just accept to be as we perceive it. How much of it is really there, and how much is a projection of our internal world. Not even necessarily literally (but who knows?). In a dream it is all you- every person, every object, every scene. It is all a facet of you. If we bring that notion into our dreams, it makes sense that we embrace it all, that we are kind to it all, and that we treat it all how we wish to be treated. If we bring that notion into our waking lives- imagine the compassionate nature, we would all have for each other.

Our dream world contains such a rich tapestry of symbols and information, yet for me it also felt as if it contained an understanding of how we show up in the world. Besides learning to wake in your dream has plenty of other benefits too. Defying the laws of being human certainly has its thrills, and you can't beat flying over the mountaintops in a nightly practice. I implore you to try it when you sleep tonight.

Create your Dream Practice - Nightly

- Create a dream diary. Tell your unconscious mind how willing you are to hear her and take a conscious interest in your dream world.
- Become aware of unusual situations when you wake, and create a dream tell, like looking at your hand and counting your fingers, or checking out the clock on the wall. Ask yourself, *'Is this a dream?'*
- Do it 10 times a day and you may find yourself asking yourself the same question at night.
- As you begin to know your dreamscape through your dream diary, you may notice something. Certain people or places show up time and again; places you haven't visited for years.
- This can become your tell, and you can say to yourself, next time I am here/see this, I know I will be dreaming.
- Set an intention before you sleep- *next time I am dreaming I will know that I am dreaming.*
- Bonus if you set an alarm an hour early and repeat that as you drift back to sleep.
- Record everything that happens in your dream time in a dedicated Dream diary that you keep by your bed

For more information check out the bibliography.

The World Woke Up

A memoir of almost anyone's life that exists in this time would not be complete without talking about 2020. Who doesn't remember where they were, how they responded, how everyone's worlds seemed to get turned upside down and inside out, where you were in the globe when the news of the pandemic hit and the fact that we were all shut inside our homes.

I appreciate the irony that this was the first year that I had actually planned out all of my monthly moon workshops, Reiki shares, angel classes and psychic development circles for the year ahead. Things were getting more popular, and hiring out the shop and having a program of classes was being called for. A local community was being born, and many of the workshops were booking out. How I loved holding the space in these different ways. Retreats were planned, talks in groups. I had never felt so on purpose, doing what I loved and reaching so many people.

Until we got the news that all premises had to shut. There is so much I could talk about in just that one month- March 2020- of how my life turned around, so let us start with this.

I knew that there was no way I was going to sit back and just let the world go by. So many were feeling lost and isolated, and I had my communities telling me how the classes were a highlight of their week. So, I asked out loud for a solution, and immediately was hit with *'Run these online'*.

At the time I had never heard of Zoom and had zero idea how to get this out there. But I didn't have anywhere else to be, and a friend suggested I try out Zoom as she had an account. So, I created an 'event' on my Facebook group and invited people to come along for a development circle. How it would work, I didn't know, but my fingers seemed to be typing before my head got in the way. Before I knew it, people were booking on.

7 in the first week turned to 10 and 15, and some gathered up to 35. I had people from all over the UK, and then branching out to mainland Europe, Canada, America and eventually into the Philippines and Australia. I was flowing and I was growing. My Spirit Team, I have to say, were on point, as I would sit and just ask in my mind what was needed and a whole plethora of workshops, discussions, meditations and courses would seemingly flow out of me.

It taught me many a lesson. How we needn't be in person to feel energies, and how they were just as powerful- if not more at times- over both time and space. How important connection and community were, in a safe space for us all to explore and understand what was going on in the world and with ourselves.

I witnessed week upon week as more and more humans were waking up to their own spirituality and power. Many were booking private sessions to help understand where this spiritual path was taking them. Before I knew it, I was often holding 4 or 5 sessions a day, plus the group programs, as well as small mentorship groups. As I grew, so did my clients. As my clients grew, so did I.

Taking so many clients, I saw first-hand the struggles we were going through as a collective. The persecution that was coming up to be healed. The energetics rising, plus the up and downside of the awakening pathway. I also connected with more teachers, with the time I had to listen to other courses and content. My mind, my experience and my vocabulary were all expanding. As the world shut down it got smaller, as communities found themselves online; like magic. And somehow, I kept being pushed by a power greater than me to keep holding space, holding steady space, whilst for so many the world fell apart.

Something happened for me as I was stepping into these holdings. It allowed me to hold space for me. During the times I was running workshops, readings and the programs, I was fully connected. Held by a power that was so beyond what I knew that it allowed me to be settled, still and assured in those moments. Yet behind the scenes, when I was alone or faced with the responsibility of three children who now weren't at school, and with the onslaught of information being thrown at me, the energetics that I too was navigating for myself, and of course all of the changes that were happening around me- the fears, the doubts, the shaky foundations… Without my practice and my work, I wonder where I would have been.

The world was closing down, whilst I was opening up. I was holding the light for many, whilst the darkness was drawing ever closer.

The words of wisdom that came through me during our sessions were as much as a help to me as they were for the client- although I didn't always know at the time. Helping people to stop dropping into fear, and process all they were going through, my guidance team shared the same with me. Knowing that there was a reason for this- that as the world shut down, the energetics were opening up. That we were shedding years of programming as things became so much more uncomfortable for so many. We were forced to slow down, and as we did, our energy sped up. The Earth was resting, and we were responding, attuning to the healing that she was receiving. I understood what a powerfully magical time it was and witnessed it all developing in front of my eyes.

All the while, my eyes were being opened in ways I could never had anticipated and most certainly never requested.

It seemed the world was going through its very own dark night of the Soul, and I felt I was right there in the eye of this imposing storm.

Through The Darkness

Something happened in many parts of the spiritual community- at least where I am- when 2020 hit. Everything that was hidden was coming to the surface. Everyone had their theories and their viewpoints. We were living in many ways through such absurdity that it was often hard to know anymore what was real and what was not. And, as we were all being pulled (sometimes kicking and screaming) out of the 3D, there was a path to cross before we got into the 5D living. The 5D where we live from our heart space, where we co-create in love with the Divine, where we are empowered sovereign beings. Where things became healed, whole, and understood. Where we met more fully our divinity

And that space was the 4D. And the 4D I found was one of the trickiest places to keep afloat.

Imagine you had two boats moving in different directions. One is the 3rd Dimension. The materialistic viewpoint of the world- it is tangible to us and so it is real. Controlled through other humans, government, and companies. We are told who we are, and we get on like good citizens doing the sleep, eat, work, play scenario over and over until we retire and maybe enjoy a little life at the end. The other is the 5th Dimension. Sovereign beings, empowered by our spirit, connected to the invisible world- the fields of love and divinity. Led by heart and soul, and all working in a collaborative light to light the way.

The 4D is like having one foot on either boat at the same time. Both pulling in different directions, and all you want to do is not fall into the turbulent sea below.

Once you start to delve in, to understand, to want to know the truth, the plasters being ripped off in one tug, over and over and over, peeling from skin that is now raw and unhealed… things compound. The algorithms feed you, people you trust send you videos with the vague *"Have you seen this?!"* Talk of the people who you thought were good were bad, and bad were good. Words like reptilians and psyops and pizza and hotdogs being thrown around the houses. High profile channellers telling you that the world is corrupt, and you can't trust anyone. Arrests, holograms and disappearing popes.

Every day I was getting at least 4 videos sent to me. Every day I was finding myself dropping down a rabbit hole of things that once you have seen, can never be unseen. 'Truths' being fed to you like delicious sweeties that you know are bad for you but are too tempting to let go of. And the deeper you go, the more absurd it got… but then if the world is run on magic, that how could we ever decipher what is actually true!?

My head was in a spin. Theories flying in. Brain kicking off. Links being made…
If ABC then it only goes to reason that XYZ....
Is that a program too?
Are the letters of the alphabet actually put together in such a way that is designed to trick you into faithful subjects of a master race that wants to eat us?

It was dangerous, thrilling, dividing and sickening all at the same time. Yet every time I thought I had reconciled something in my head, another theory, another viewpoint, another channel, another respected teacher said something else. Whilst it was all just theory, it was one thing. When it started to affect decisions, when it started to cause debate and rejection with loved ones, enough was enough.

Every day I would have someone else reach out to me and want answers. *What did I think to this video that was released? What should one do about this medical intervention? What am I going to do about my health choices*? Like I had all the answers! I didn't, I was still trying to figure it out for myself. Discernment was getting harder and harder, and I no longer knew which sources I could trust and rely on.

Apart from one. When I was holding space and energy, words of wisdom would flow out of me. A neutrality, a stability to reassure, and remind those of what is truly important. To keep falling back into love. I realise now it was a reminder for me, yet when faced with this onslaught of information, it was tough. And much of it was very disturbing. Yet somehow, I found the strength- eventually- to crawl out of the rabbit holes I had been down for months. I could see where they were leading, and it wasn't nice. However, 'true' they were, whatever nuggets of information they hold, regardless of how they showed me the 'real' inner workings of the world, I came to a decision.

If it was causing separation, if it was causing one to judge and fall out of love, if it was causing one to blame, shame or reject another human… then it wasn't one for me. Do I regret the hours of 'research' in the name of 'truth'? The hours I walked and listened to others? Following the links which led to another and another? No, I don't. Are there things that I wish I could un-see…? Perhaps. Yet somehow, I needed to drop into that all. I needed to look deep into me and understand where I held that; where I resonated with what was being shown; where I turned my head and ignored things that were uncomfortable or downright wrong; where I complied or did things just because I was told; and where I had fallen into programming. Also, where I draw my boundaries and where I allow for something outside of me, that I can never know for sure which is real or not, to influence, upset and disjoin me.

It was important for me to change my focus. To help me instead find stability and a grounding. To trust in my connection when so much around me was telling me it wasn't safe to trust. To help me find the light in the darkness so I could help others do the same. To honour where everyone around me was, despite their view of the world, the decisions they made and what they believed. To ensure that my role was not to seep others in fear, but to help them return to love, as I did for myself.

If anything, it taught me something very important. Tolerance. Compassion. Understanding. Seeing, even in my own family where views so different to my own were passionately presented. People I loved, who loved me, that were so deep in their own opinions and their own understanding of what was happening. I realised that it was up to me to find that middle ground. To be the one who knew that, even when views were at polar ends of the scale, that it didn't make anyone good/bad, right/wrong, better/best or worse. It was simply a view.

Of course, it comes up that we want to be right, but with so much I had learned, believed, rejected, accepted, *right* was probably the last thing I wanted to be. I decided I would rather choose peace than choose righteousness, and that was a huge lesson for me. Watching when I wanted to defend, battle, or attack. When I wanted to retreat and hide. When I became flustered or overwhelmed. When I was in defiance. And most of all, when I was in judgement. Judgement of me, of others, of all that was going on. All I knew was that I didn't *know*. I could just feel. So that was what I did, I felt through it all, and endeavoured to be the stability for others.

Moving into 5D, certainly isn't about 'being right'. Moving into 5D is about being aware of the invisible world, connecting in with what we cannot see, or know for sure. Seeing beyond the material form. Having an awareness of our higher selves and allowing for that aspect of us to influence and guide. Finding and encouraging new ways of living, of being. Showing up from the heart. Moving away from 'seeing is believing' and knowing that believing is seeing. Living in the 5D is neither about being 'Woke' or 'Conspiratorial' but being aware of it all and still choosing Love. Coming back into self. Healing the trauma that arises. Taking responsibility. Having eyes to see, but not judge. Taking responsibility of your words, your thoughts, your actions. The dramas that are playing out, all of you are witnessing. All of it. And still, always, each and every time, returning to love.

And no one ever said that would be easy, however simple it may sound.

The Attack

Energy attracts energy; it has to. So, the months I spent diving down the rabbit holes, immersed in an underworld of activity, had in many ways taken its toll. Lucky for me, I had my practices keeping me buoyant in these choppy waters, but one day- tired, lazy perhaps, and having followed clickbait after another of 'interviews' and 'documentaries' shared with me that left my jaw hanging- I went to bed with no intention other than to sleep.

I am used to my dreams informing me, and I am lucky to experience very vivid dreams which I often remember. However, this one night, my dreams were flitting forward and backwards, like I was in an old movie with flashbacks and flash-forwards that were leaving me very disorientated, even in the dream state. At some point in the middle of the night, I awoke to this very strange sound in my ear. It sounded like morse code- *beep bep be beep beep.* I could hear it outside of my head, and it sounded nothing like the Angel download high frequency ringing I was so used to experiencing. I remember thinking,

"*What is that? That's not right,*" before drifting back to sleep.

The next morning, I awoke with only a vague recollection of what happened. But I felt off. Instinctively, when I got in the shower, I cupped a handful of Dead Sea and Himalayan salts with some essential oils of Mugwort and Frankincense, and a little dried lavender and scrubbed my body. This helped, I felt a little lighter, but I also had this really weird feeling like my energy had been capped. I was tired and I had a day of clients ahead of me. I went to write, and my words wouldn't come out. All I could think about was one of the videos I had been watching the night before with those images and quite absurd claims hanging in my mind.

It was like I had lost my mojo, and I felt myself sinking. How lucky I was to have a chance phone call with the Shaman where I remembered what had happened with the morse code and shared it with her. Right away we identified what it was, and set to cleaning my energy body, bringing in the light and renouncing all that had come in, that somehow- knowingly or not- I had allowed in. It took a tonne of water, a heap of energetic practices and a long walk-in nature to bring me back into some equilibrium, but boy, was it a reminder for me. Where I put my energy is the most precious resource I have. Where I direct my consciousness literally creates my reality. And like does indeed attract like. That was the moment I decided no more. Yes, of course, be aware. Be open to information. Do not bury my head in the sand, but be discerning as to what I listen to, who I listen to and how much I listen.

And it seemed it worked. Less and less messages were coming in my inbox. I reset the algorithm on both my social media and my energy vortex, to more uplifting and Soul affirming channels. I declared my intention once again. To serve my source. And I moved on from the darkness that was trying to grip me.

In awareness. Eyes open. Observing, not absorbing. In compassion. In grace. In understanding. Connecting to Heaven and to Earth. Open to the highest sources of wisdom. A hand had somehow reached down and grabbed me, propelling me somewhere:

Into 5D, and wow the view from up here is so much more... inspiring.

The Deep Dive

As my one-to-one practices were growing, often doing 4 guidance sessions or Akashic Readings a day, my energy was growing and expanding. The complexity of the people I was working with was growing, and I knew that it was only right for me to grow in my skills. Plus, I was itching to learn more.

Reading through a newsletter that was sent to me, a course I saw got all the feels going in my body. Soul Transformation Therapy. I knew nothing about it, but just the short paragraph I read, plus a huge pull from my solar plexus led me to signing up pretty much immediately. The course was phenomenal. Blending Eastern and Western Psycho-spiritual interventions, channelled symbols based on the Hebrew alphabet that I was so familiar with, channellings and tapping, and parts work and intuition. I knew within the first hour that something special was happening.

I connected with the course tutor, Blue Marsden, shortly after and asked him what the next step was. That was what led me to enrol on the biggest course I had done since my degree- a 16-month Spiritual Counselling Diploma. Each module focusing on different aspects that we could use to help our clients. Too many to list out here, but we covered so much including Energy Psychology, Hypnotherapy, Grief, Astrology, Counselling Skills, Communication… Oh, I was in my element. But who knew that this would be so much more than learning? Who knew that so much of the beauty of this was discovering more about myself? Thinking I was in a good place, and often not knowing what to work on, each session would lead to a deep healing or unearthing of another layer that was ready to come up. Over and over again, month upon month. Not only learning more about how to hold space for others, processes that blended intuitive knowing with energy, with psychologically backed interventions, but also holding space for me, which in turn created more space within.

I couldn't even tell you which ones I enjoyed the most. Each encounter with myself simply helped me to know more about who I am. And as I grew, the space I held grew, and as the space I held grew, so did my capacity to help.

We hold so many layers. I am not sure that this path will ever lead to an end. Our psychology, our Karma, our Soul. Our Human, our Path, our Future. Our self, our Other, our Selves. Whatever we focus on, our energy brings more to. As we focus on healing, it brings to us all that needs to be healed. As we heal, we do not heal alone. We heal our ancestors, our descendants, the collective consciousness, the world.

The more I delved into the psychology, the more important the spirituality became. This gave us the purpose of the work we are doing. The intention to rise, and evolve, and grow. The pull to live a life of purpose. To connect with others. To earn our full badge in our designated colour of this lifetime- diving deep into the depths of all this frequency had on offer for us, so opening us up to the rest of the spectrum for us to continue in the evolution that is Soul.

This was not digging deep for the sake of it. Not rehashing all traumas to find sense. This is us truly knowing ourselves. Truly becoming. Whole. One. True.

The Sum Of The Parts

There's nothing more frustrating than wanting to consciously do something, yet you find yourself sabotaging yourself, being pulled in different directions, or finding yourself behaving in the exact opposite way than you had intended to in the first place. I couldn't always understand it. For you see, I believe that our body follows our mind, yet so often it is the other way round. I mean, if you think about doing something or going somewhere- well you have the thought and then the body takes you to where you are thinking of… right? Yet sometimes, the body has a very compelling feeling or reaction that then makes you change your mind and do something else.

I have often wondered where it is our thoughts come in the first place, and I spoke about this in earlier chapters. We certainly don't work *alone,* and we can tap into many other conscious awareness's that surround us.

But what about what is *within* us?

I think therefore I am…?

Which begs the question, who and what am I?

Daughter, Mother, Wife, Sister.
Teacher, Student, Mentor, Writer.
Female, Entrepreneur, Jewish, Spiritual?
Pisces, Manifesting Generator, ENTJ.
Brunette, Woman, Homeowner, Business Owner, Taxpayer?

What about the stories we have told ourselves, and the things we have identified with? What about our past life traumas? What about our humanness, our spiritualness, our Starseed origins? What about the way we experience ourselves in the world? What about all the other labels put upon us that we may not even know about yet?

All of them. Each and every single one of them, consciously or not are playing a role. Influencing us and guiding us.

I realise quite how many different roles I identified with. How many labels had been placed upon me or by me. And there were so many times they were all there, having different opinions and infighting.

Like the 100s of times I thought about writing this very book you are reading… yet a part of me told me the words would never come. Like the times I wanted to speak up and right a wrong, yet a part of me told me that wasn't safe to do so. Like the times I wanted to eat healthily, yet a part of me needed the comfort that only food seemed to bring.

All of these different parts of me were playing a role. The victim showing up when I wanted to blame the world for things not always going my way. Or the martyr calling the shots when I was too proud to ask for help. Or the inner child throwing a strop when I felt rejected or not listened to. Or the protector stepping into stop me allowing anyone to get any closer than they already were.

Sometimes it felt like there was a battle going on right there in my head. A committee all set up that couldn't agree, which left me feeling frazzled and confused.

That was until I met them, those parts. The moment I realised that all of these parts of me were active, that they weren't me... but they were living breathing *parts* of me, things started to change. I learned how to give them voice. I let them say their piece and let them be heard. I discovered that my protector was only trying to keep me safe because I was afraid of my own power. I discovered that my heart's guardian was there to stop me getting stabbed in the back once again. I understood that the victim in me was scared of doing something wrong and didn't want to get punished. And I became aware that the mystic in me was so powerful that in the past it had left me burned.

Most importantly, I identified that not one of these identities were out to harm me. Quite the opposite. They all wanted to protect me. They all wanted what they thought was best for me, based on experiences they had in the past. They were all somehow put there by me so that I would fit in, stay alive, allow me to keep my identity (*there's an irony there I am sure*), and keep a purpose and meaning in my life. Yet there had never been a time that I had allowed them to all come onboard and express themselves. Which, of course, led them to an inner battle.

Now, my initial thought was to go ahead and abandon all the destructive ones, of course. After all, for me it was about living a Soul-led life. Being bossed around by my inner diva was not congruent with that.

Turns out, that wasn't the best way. Turned out that, as I turned away, these parts began to shout louder. As I put other more *'acceptable'* parts of me in charge, these parts that were ignored went into survival mode and threw all their toys out of the pram, showing up when I least expected or needed it. Turned out that all they needed was to be seen, heard, voiced, and reassured that things were safe. And even *(gasp)* being asked for their opinion.

Turned out that was a better way to navigate this. And so, I did. As I did so, something very interesting happened.

I realised that I am not my voice. I realised that I am not my mind. I realised that I am not the victim, or the martyr, or the warrior, or the mystic. I realised that I am the observer of each of them. That I am the one that empowers or disempowers them, and that it is always up to me to choose which one I take advice from.

I discovered that as I took their advice, and then asked Soul to guide me as to which are the best decisions to make, I no longer needed all of them as identities.

For I am not the sum of my parts. I am not what I think. I just AM.

Whole. Sovereign. Free

The Embrace

Embracing who you are is the best way forward. But how hard is it when you don't truly know who or what that is? The potentials, the pitfalls, the sensitivities, the likes, the dislikes, the aversions, the draws. I had enough of numbing it out, of pretending. There was no point to do that. I am here and I was put on this Earth to be me in my fullest.

What did I know about myself at this time? That I was stronger than I thought. That I had potential to help others transform. That people felt comfortable with me, and that I was able to make them feel safe. That I now, felt safe in myself.

I knew that I had a potential, that we all did. I knew that the things that I most wanted to turn away from were the things that held the most healing for me. And I knew that, if I had the courage to turn towards them, that this was where the magic is. I learned that I tried to avoid it as often as possible, but when I finally allowed myself to, learned that I was strong enough to do that too.

I knew that I wasn't meant to be following a path that was already laid out for me, and I knew that carving a path from scratch is never easy. I knew that what I do is always find the path of least resistance. That I was like water in that way. I knew that often, I was the very resistance that challenged me so much. I knew that I liked to be different, and that I also liked to be liked, but those things didn't need to be mutually exclusive. I knew that I didn't have to 'make' myself different, I just was, in fact we all are, and that was OK. I learned I had this perfectionist streak in me that wants everything to be just so, but then I let things come through me that I could never possibly plan. I knew also that that was often scary. I knew that I had done a tonne of healing on myself, and that quite possibly there was a tonne more. I knew that as I showed up for others, I also showed up for myself. As I showed up for myself, I also showed up for others.

I knew that I didn't gravitate towards many of the things that others did. That the latest movie, show, gossip or celebrity didn't really interest me much. I knew that when I did watch a movie or a series, I would feel the characters as myself, and that was overwhelming sometimes. I learned that music could make my body go on high alert, but other music could soothe me instantly. I learned that I was best off focusing on things that my brain could consider and explore, that were life affirming and deep- like quantum physics, or the inner workings of a philosophy- because if it doesn't, well then it would go on doing that for all the woes in the world. I knew that I wasn't the many identities I put upon myself and that were put on me. And I knew that I wanted nothing more than to be me. Free.

So, I claimed it all. As I did, it claimed me less. My faults, my masks, my shadows, my gold, my smile, my potential. It was all valid and all a part of me, but me? Me. I was so much more.

Embracing myself. Allowing myself to be human. Fallible. Raw. Vulnerable. Strong. Empathic. Intelligent. Intuitive. Sensitive. Even Angry. Overwhelmed. Whatever showed, I learned to love that too.

I allowed myself to be seen then. No more hiding away. I wrote and shared with whoever would listen, that which I really felt and saw and thought. I came fully out the spiritual closet. I allowed myself to lead. Lead myself first. And others came, so together we could all lead this new way of being. This was my journey, and finally, finally, I was ready to embrace it as my own.

So, I did. Sometimes it was messy. Sometimes it was beautiful. Sometimes it made no sense, and sometimes I felt alone. But most of the time I was reassured. Reassured by this deep, deep knowing that was so much bigger than me. That allowed me to trust in something more. To trust more in myself. To allow myself to lead. To create my community and be right there with them, there in the centre, holding space.

I allowed myself to travel down a path that I didn't know, that I hadn't seen, that had forged before me.

And that path has led me right here. With you now. Reading these words. Feeling this energy. With the hope that knowing me, as I am, as I was, and as I continue to grow and forge the way, has helped you to know yourself better. So that you can allow, and know, and grow. Giving yourself permission to fail and rise. To stop and to start. To live and to love. To doubt and to trust. To simply be you and who you are. In all the magnificent messiness we know ourselves to be.

Perhaps, reading this helps you to see the truth of the light that you are. That inside each and every thought, decision, action and awareness- the whole universe resides. And so, you have the potential of the whole universe inside you.

Perhaps you know. That you are me, and I am you. That we are each our own facet of the same crystal, or our own star in the same constellation, or our unique note in the same melody. And that all you can do, all that any of us can do, is endeavour to face, or shine, or sing in the highest expression of ourselves.

Perhaps you too know yourself to be your very own mystic in training.

Perhaps, this is where your story begins.

May your journey be one you cherish.

Melissa x

Let's Keep In Touch

If you're interested in following as my journey continues to unfold, find me on social media @TheMelissaAmos

Please visit my author page on Amazon to share your experiences and reviews. Thank you

A library of meditations and practices to compliment the concepts in this book can be found at https://melissa-amos.com/mystics or following this QR code

Visit melissa-amos.com/mystics for support materials

A Note From The Author

There's a vulnerability that comes with writing a book, and having it out in the world. Others, that you have never met before reading your words and knowing you, on a level deeper than perhaps many friends and family may know. Now you have read my words, journeyed with me, heard my story, my hope is that it has imparted something upon you.

I know, through my own learnings and teachings, that where I have learned and grown the most is where my teachers have so graciously shared, without censorship or withdrawal all they knew. So I knew, when writing this, it will be all or nothing. As someone who appreciates her privacy, and has spent her life recoiling from taking up space in certain environments whilst growing in comfort in others, it is both liberating and nerving to know these words are now in your hand.

I am just a regular girl, on a quest, on her own journey. Isn't that true for all of us? So, to the teachers that have shared with me, to all those that have helped me learn lessons, both enjoyable and otherwise, I give my heartfelt gratitude and thanks. And mostly to you. For supporting yourself and knowing that there may indeed be some magic in the world, and starting where it all needs to happen. Right there with you.

Bibliography

Whilst the combinations and concepts that have been shared in this book has come from my unique understanding of the world, many of the ideas have been drawn from many books, summits, podcasts and courses I have learned along the way.

I would love to give credit to these Authors for inspiring me with their wisdom and guidance. Should you feel drawn, you may wish to embark in your own journey of understanding with these suggestions.

Robert Holden and Louise Hay: Life Loves You
Blue Marsden: Soul Plan
Kyle Gray: Angel Prayers & Divine Masters, Ancient Wisdom Plus, I highly recommend his card decks
Charlie Morley: Dreaming through Darkness & Dreams of Awakening.
Wayne Dyer: Choose from a large library
Barbel Mohr: The Cosmic Ordering Service
Jane Roberts: The Seth Series
Abraham Hicks: Ask and It is Given
Greg Braden: The Divine Matrix & The God Code
Rhonda Byrne: The Secret
Dr David Hamilton: How your Mind Can Heal Your Body
Linda Howe: Discover Your Souls Path
Alberto Villoldo: How To Grow A New Body
James Redfield: The Celestine Prophecy

Acknowledgements

As well as the vast reading list above, and each of the Authors and Teachers that have shared so generously with me, I would like to give particular thanks to the following:

Molly-Ann Smith. My Nana, my mentor, my inspiration for writing this book. Before she passed away in 2020 she began to make notes for her own book, which she titled; The High Notes. A lifelong dream of hers to get published, you may notice her words which weave through the fabric of this book

My entire family, Mum, Dad, Adam. Particularly My husband Mark. Who supported me through all of this, the journey before, during and beyond, and each bedtime with the kids whilst I was writing this book deep into the night. His support literally like the roots of my tree so I could be free to reach and grow and discover.

Max, Kai and Coby. I love you with all my heart, my mind and my Soul

Soul Space. My inner community. Each of you are a light in my life, and Mystics in your own right. Thank you for all your support and continuing to be there through the crazy and whacky ideas.

For supporting me with this book, my editor Katie Oman, for encouraging and advising, and reading and rereading and reading again!

To Laura Mitchell whose Soul makes a song of life, and who has provided all the sound medicine in the accompanying meditations and journeys.

Of course to Jessica Paschke and Ioanna Schiza, the very first readers of these words, for your honesty and guidance, and to Sushmita Jain and Desislava Dobreva, for being there and helping me make this a reality. Blue Marsden, and Robert Holden plus all the pre-release readers of the book for the encouragement and support.

To my teachers, all of those mentioned in these words, and all of those that have influenced, encouraged, shared and questioned. Without your openness and guidance, it would have taken a whole lot longer.

Clair Dean Daws, you saw me before I did. My Reiki teachers, starting with Michele Hancock, for opening me into this world. Pauline Wing for trusting me in your circle and taking me a step further along this path, and each of you who sat in circle with me, week upon week. Grant, Golden Paw for holding space with me time and again. The Shaman, for all you taught me. Willa for opening my records and everything since.

The healers who have held space for me whilst embarking on this writing journey. Shi XingFa and Annette Graham, and my yoga teachers, particularly Jackie Jones for keeping me moving, flowing and growing.

And to each and every one of you that has bought, read, shared, reviewed and loved this book. Thank you for helping me create this legacy.

I love you all

Notes

You've got this!

Love Melissa
X